Wage Growth in the Civilian Careers of Military Retirees

David S. Loughran

Prepared for the
Office of the Secretary of Defense

National Defense Research Institute

RAND

The research described in this report was sponsored by the Office of the Secretary of Defense (OSD). The research was conducted in RAND's National Defense Research Institute, a federally funded research and development center supported by the OSD, the Joint Staff, the unified commands, and the defense agencies under Contract DASW01-95-C-0059.

Library of Congress Cataloging-in-Publication Data

Loughran, David S., 1969-
    Wage growth in the civilian careers of military retirees / David S. Loughran.
    p. cm.
    "MR-1363."
    Includes bibliographical references.
    ISBN 0-8330-3058-2
    1. Retired military personnel—Employment—United States. 2. Retired military personnel—Salaries, etc.—United States. I. Title.

UB443 .L68 2001
331.2'973'08697—dc21

2001048379

RAND is a nonprofit institution that helps improve policy and decisionmaking through research and analysis. RAND® is a registered trademark. RAND's publications do not necessarily reflect the opinions or policies of its research sponsors.

Published 2002 by RAND
1700 Main Street, P.O. Box 2138, Santa Monica, CA 90407-2138
1200 South Hayes Street, Arlington, VA 22202-5050
201 North Craig Street, Suite 102, Pittsburgh, PA 15213-1516
RAND URL: http://www.rand.org/
To order RAND documents or to obtain additional information, contact Distribution Services: Telephone: (310) 451-7002; Fax: (310) 451-6915; Email: order@rand.org

More than 20,000 individuals retire each year from the U.S. military who are eligible to receive a guaranteed annuity amounting to half or more of their basic military pay. Separating from the military at an average age of 43, the overwhelming majority of these retirees enter second careers in the civilian sector. This book seeks to answer three questions about the civilian labor market experience of military retirees: (1) How do the wages of military retirees upon separation compare with those of comparably experienced and educated civilians?; (2) Do military retirees enjoy higher relative wage growth over their second careers than their civilian peers?; and (3) Is the transition to civilian employment a difficult process for military retirees?

Using a novel data set on military retirees—the 1996 Survey of Retired Military Personnel (SRMP)—this study finds that military retirees earn substantially lower wages than their civilian peers upon entering the civilian labor market. This finding holds even after controlling for a range of observable differences between military retirees and civilians. Moreover, this study finds that the wages of military retirees remain low relative to civilian wages even as they gain civilian labor market experience. While the study cannot tell us whether the low relative wages of military retirees is due to military service itself, the effect of retirement pay on effort exerted in the civilian labor market, or other unobserved differences between military retirees and civilians, it does provide a more complete picture of the civilian experience of military retirees than was previously available. The results of this study will be useful to readers who are thinking about the military retirement system as a force-shaping tool and those who are concerned more generally about the welfare of military retirees in their civilian lives.

This study was conducted under the sponsorship of the Director of the 9th Quadrennial Review of Military Compensation (QRMC) in the Office of the Under Secretary of Defense for Personnel and Readiness. It was prepared within the Forces and Resources Policy Center of RAND's National Defense Research Institute (NDRI), a federally funded research and development center sponsored by the Office of the Secretary of Defense, the Joint Staff, the unified commands, and the defense agencies.

CONTENTS

FIGURES

TABLES

More than 20,000 individuals retire each year from the U.S. military who are eligible to receive a guaranteed annuity amounting to half or more of their basic military pay. Separating from the military at an average age of 43, the overwhelming majority of these retirees enter second careers in the civilian sector. For a variety of reasons, one might expect military retirees to enter the civilian labor force earning wages lower than what comparable civilians earn. The most frequently cited reason for this is that military training does not transfer perfectly to civilian occupations and therefore retirees must enter a period of training upon separation before their wages can be expected to catch up with those of their civilian peers. Whereas the post-service earnings of veterans in general have received a great deal of attention in the economics literature, much of this literature focuses on veterans serving for one or two terms of enlistment only. Comparatively little research, prior to this study, has examined the civilian labor market experience of military retirees who, by definition, have completed a minimum of 20 years of service.

STUDY QUESTIONS

This study seeks to answer three questions about the civilian labor market experience of military retirees: (1) How do the wages of military retirees upon separation compare with those of comparably experienced and educated civilians?; (2) Do military retirees enjoy higher relative wage growth over their second careers than their civilian peers?; and (3) Is the transition to civilian employment a difficult process for military retirees?

Obtaining answers to these questions is important for a variety of reasons. First, the success of military compensation policy hinges on the civilian earnings potential of prospective and active military personnel. This is particularly true in the case of the military pension system, one of the military's most significant force-shaping tools. By deferring some compensation, the military pension system creates an incentive for the most-talented individuals to stay in the military and seek promotion and for the least-talented individuals, those who doubt they can achieve the requisite rank and longevity, to separate voluntarily early in their careers. This deferred compensation also motivates work effort because up-or-out rules require those who choose to stay in the military to continue advancing in rank.

The effectiveness of the military pension system in accomplishing this type of "self-sorting" depends on many factors. Chief among those factors is how additional years of service affect civilian earnings potential. In general, one can expect a given annuity to be less successful in retaining high-quality personnel if years of service (YOS) has a negative causal effect on civilian earnings. While this study does not definitively answer how military service affects the civilian earnings of military retirees, it does provide a more complete picture of the civilian experience of military retirees than was previously available.

STUDY RESULTS

As did earlier research, this study finds, using several data sets including the 1996 Survey of Retired Military Personnel (SRMP), that the relative civilian earnings of retirees in 1995 are substantially higher among those who separated in the 1970s than among those who separated in the 1990s. This study also finds, however, that the relative earnings of retirees upon separation from the military have fallen with successive cohorts. Together, these two facts imply a low level of relative wage growth for retirees over the course of their civilian careers.

This conclusion contrasts with the findings of earlier research suggesting that military retirees who enter the civilian labor market with below-average wages tend to catch up with their civilian peers after five to ten years in the civilian labor market (Borjas and Welch, 1986; Cardell et al., 1997). This difference in findings is attributed to the failure of earlier research to control for cohort effects, which can bias cross-sectional estimates of relative wage growth. The findings from this study are also contrary to the predictions of a simple human capital model in which high returns to investment in civilian skills among military retirees cause them to accumulate civilian skills at a faster rate than their civilian peers, thereby leading to higher relative wage growth. Assuming this lack of relative wage growth in the retiree population continues in the future, one can expect the wages of recent military retirees to lag behind those of their civilian peers throughout their civilian careers.

Whether one should be surprised that military retirees, especially those retiring most recently, earn substantially less than their civilian peers depends in large part on whether one believes that this study has chosen an appropriate peer group. It may be that, even conditional on observable characteristics, important differences remain in both the labor market ability of retirees and civilians and the effort they expend in the civilian labor market that drive observed differences in civilian earnings. Formally controlling for unobserved differences in ability and effort is beyond the scope of this research.

Nevertheless, this research does make use of a variety of questions in the SRMP that seem to suggest that observed differences in wages between retirees and civilians are less a function of ability than they are a function of effort. For example, whereas 70 percent of the retirees separating between 1990 and 1994 earn wages below median civilian wages (conditional on age and education), only 30 percent reported feeling that their military career hindered their chance of earning wages comparable to those of their civilian peers. This suggests their peer group may also earn less than median wages. Moreover, 91 percent of respondents report being satisfied with their civilian life and 90 percent report being satisfied with their military career. It is doubtful that these retirees would report such high levels of satisfaction if they thought their civilian wages were lagging far behind those of their peers.

Also of note is the fact that restricting the comparison to retirees and other veterans does little to alter the results of the analysis. That is, the same pattern in relative retiree wages is observed if the civilian comparison group is restricted to just veterans. In so doing, one presumably controls for factors that led both retirees and veterans with less than 20 years of service to enlist in the military in the first place (for example, both populations perceived the military to be a better opportunity than the civilian labor market when they first enlisted). Clearly, there remain important unobserved differences between retirees and other veterans, but controlling for veteran status perhaps reduces the scope for large differences in labor market ability to drive the differences observed in civilian wages.

Military retirees' access to pension income could affect their supply of effort in the labor market. In theory, this pension income would tend to cause retirees to consume more leisure, whether it be in the form of fewer work hours or less effort on the job, than their civilian peers. Indeed, when pension income is added to retiree wages, the gap between retiree and civilian earnings disappears. This may help explain why nearly 80 percent of retirees report that they are doing as well or better economically than their civilian peers despite the fact that nearly 60 percent earn wages substantially below median civilian wages.

Differences in effort could also help explain why the study does not show the wages of retirees catching up with civilian wages as retirees gain civilian labor market experience. The availability of pension income, for example, might influence not only the type of job retirees initially select, but also their motivation to excel in that job and advance beyond their civilian peers. Hence, pension income could affect not only the initial level of retiree wages but the relative growth in retiree wages as well.

Perhaps the most surprising and potentially troubling finding is that the relative wages of retirees have fallen across successive cohorts of retirees. There is little evidence that the quality of military retirees has changed dramatically over time, so declining worker quality does not seem to be a plausible explanation for the deteriorating relative position of retirees. Other possibilities are that the relative return to civilian experience vis-à-vis military experience increased between 1970 and 1994. Retirees separating in the early 1970s could secure jobs with wages that were comparable to civilian wages because their military experience earned the same return as civilian experience. By the early 1990s the same level of military experience earned a lower relative return and therefore one observes retirees separating at that time earning wages well below mean civilian wages.

Another possibility for the relative decline of retiree wages is that more-recent retirees are more likely to make civilian employment decisions in concert with the employment choices of their spouses. The rate of female labor force participation rose sharply between 1970 and 1994 and therefore the likelihood that a given retiree's labor market choices would be constrained by a spouse's career has no doubt risen as well. If a retiree is no longer viewed as a household's primary earner, the retiree may be more likely to settle for a relatively low paying job and contribute more time to household production. Spousal income might also generate a wealth effect that causes more-recent retirees to consume more leisure time. This report offers no direct evidence on either of these hypotheses, but suggests they may deserve more detailed consideration in future research.

IMPLICATIONS

In the end, this research does not say whether the military has set its current annuity at an optimal level, but it does suggest that retirees, at least, find it to be an adequate benefit. Total earnings (civilian wages plus pension income) of retirees is comparable to their prior military earnings and exceeds the mean earnings of their civilian peers. Whether the annuity is set too low in the sense that the military loses high-ability individuals early on to civilian careers, or too high in the sense that it overcompensates retirees relative to their civilian opportunities is a more complicated question that must await further research.

ACKNOWLEDGMENTS

This report has benefited enormously from the detailed reviews of RAND colleagues Beth Asch, James Hosek, and Robert Schoeni. Their many helpful comments and insights made important contributions to the analysis presented herein. I am equally indebted to John Warner and John Enns for their thoughtful reviews of earlier drafts of this report. I also extend thanks to members of the 9th Quadrennial Review of Military Compensation who provided useful suggestions in the early stages of this research. Finally, many thanks to Claudia Szabo who assisted in preparing an earlier version of this document and Nancy DelFavero for her editing work on the final report.

AFQT	Armed Forces Qualifying Test
CPS	Current Population Survey
DoD	Department of Defense
DMDC	Defense Manpower Data Center
DRS	Department of Defense Retirement Survey
FTYR	Full-Time Year-Round
FY	Fiscal Year
IV	Instrumental Variable
JMPS	Joint Uniform Military Pay System
NBER	National Bureau of Economic Research
OLS	Ordinary Least Squares
PSEHF	Post-Service Earnings History File
PSID	Panel Study of Income Dynamics
QRMC	Quadrennial Review of Military Compensation
SRMP	Survey of Retired Military Personnel
YOR	Year of Retirement
YOS	Years of Service

Chapter One

INTRODUCTION

Between 1990 and 1994, an average of 26,000 individuals retired each year from the U.S. military with 20 or more years of service. Separating from the military at an average age of 43, the overwhelming majority of these retirees are just entering their prime earning years. The civilian earnings of full-time employed males, for example, tend to peak when those individuals are in their early 50s. For a variety of reasons, though, we might expect military retirees to enter the civilian labor force earning wages that are lower than what comparable civilian workers earn. The most frequently cited reason for this wage difference is that military training does not transfer perfectly to civilian occupations and therefore retirees must enter a period of training upon separation before their wages can be expected to catch up with those of their civilian peers. Whereas the post-service earnings of veterans in general have received a great deal of attention in the economics literature, much of this literature focuses on veterans serving for one or two terms of enlistment only. Comparatively little research examines the civilian labor market experience of military retirees who, by definition, have served a minimum of 20 years.

Research on the post-service earnings of veterans is motivated in large part by the idea that the decision to enter and remain in the military is a function of outside civilian labor market opportunities. The success of military compensation policy hinges on the civilian earnings potential of prospective and active military personnel. This is particularly true in the case of the military pension system, which provides an immediate and guaranteed inflation-adjusted annuity to all military retirees. Currently, this annuity amounts to half or more of basic pay in the final years of service (an average of $16,500 in 1995).[1]

In aggregate terms, the military pension system is substantial. In 1995, roughly 1.6 million military retirees received military pension payments totaling more than $26 billion. These payments represented 9.5 percent of total U.S. defense spending and just under 40 percent of annual compensation paid to active and inactive duty personnel (Department of Defense, 1996).[2] While the number of new retirees entering the retirement system is not likely to rise appreciably in the coming years, the total number of retirees receiving pension payments is likely to continue its long-term trend upward given the general decline in mortality rates among older Americans.[3]

As Asch and Warner (1994) point out, the purpose of the military pension system is not so much to provide a vehicle for tax-sheltered savings or to facilitate a smooth transition to civilian life as it is a means of retaining high-quality personnel. The military is constrained by its inability to hire individuals from outside the organization to fill senior positions (the so-called lateral-entry constraint). The upper echelons of the military hierarchy must be filled by individuals moving up through the ranks. One way for the military to identify individuals with the requisite skills necessary to perform high-level tasks in the military is to create a compensation system that provides incentives for individuals to "self-sort" according to ability.

The military pension, by deferring a portion of compensation, creates an incentive for the most-talented individuals to stay in the military and seek promotion and for the least-talented individuals, those who doubt they can achieve the requisite rank and longevity, to separate voluntarily early in their careers. This deferred compensation also motivates work effort because up-or-out rules require those who

---

[1]Computation of active-duty retirement pay varies by date of entry into military service (before September 8, 1980, between September 9, 1980, and July 31, 1986, and after July 31, 1986). In this study, all retirees entered prior to 1980.

[2]U.S. defense spending totaled $272 billion in 1995 and regular military compensation totaled $40 billion.

[3]The total number of individuals receiving retired pay has increased steadily from 0.9 million in 1972 to 1.6 million in 1995.

choose to stay to continue advancing in rank (Asch and Warner, 1994). By encouraging self-sorting through deferred compensation, the military can avoid to a large extent the need to involuntarily separate individuals from the military. Involuntary separation, while entirely legal, could become quite costly by adversely affecting morale—individuals may perceive the prospect of involuntary separation as both risky and unfair—and encouraging individuals to lobby against the policy (Milgrom, 1988).

Other deferred compensation strategies, such as the use of retention bonuses, can also accomplish self-sorting. The pension system, however, may be a particularly desirable form of deferred compensation. One advantage of the pension system is that it creates increasingly strong incentives to leave the military after 20 years of service. The military wants to maintain a relatively youthful corps and keep the opportunity for advancement among junior personnel reasonably high by separating even the most-productive individuals soon after they are vested at 20 years of service.

At the time of vesting, individuals must weigh the benefits of separating and accepting an immediate annuity today against the benefits in terms of a higher future annuity of accruing additional years of service and possibly higher rank. Because years of service have a relatively small impact on the value of the annuity and the prospects for further advancement diminish significantly with tenure, the financial value of remaining in the military beyond 20 years of service does not rise appreciably with additional years of service, and for some service members may actually fall. Indeed, 53 percent of eligible enlisted personnel accept retirement at 20 years of service; by 22 years of service, 52 percent of eligible officers accept retirement.[4]

Whereas the basic structure of the military pension system seems well designed, in theory at least, to encourage the type of self-sorting the military desires, it is not clear that the magnitude of the annuity is set at an optimal level. The optimal level of the annuity will depend on many factors. Chief among them is how additional years of service affect civilian earnings potential. In general, we can expect a

---

[4]Officers tend to separate somewhat later because their opportunity for advancement is higher.

given annuity to be less successful in retaining high-quality personnel if longer military service itself reduces future civilian earnings.

An extensive empirical literature in economics and elsewhere has attempted to estimate the effect of military service on subsequent civilian earnings with mixed results.[5] The ambiguity comes in modeling which individuals choose to reenlist or separate. Unobservable characteristics that determine both reenlistment and subsequent civilian earnings can bias our interpretation of the correlation between military service and earnings. A number of papers in the literature attempt to control for unobservable characteristics, such as labor market ability, using instrumental variables (IVs) and selection-correction methods. This evidence suggests that military service diminishes the civilian earnings potential of veterans (Angrist 1989, 1990, and 1998; Angrist and Krueger, 1994), although some studies looking at the post-Vietnam era have found modest wage premiums for specific groups of veterans (Gilroy et al., 1992; Bryant et al., 1993; Goldberg and Warner, 1987).[6]

This report makes no attempt to model the unobservable determinants of reenlistment and wages and therefore cannot say whether military service has a causal effect on earnings. My goal here is more descriptive in nature. Specifically, this study seeks to answer three questions: (1) How do the wages of military retirees upon separation compare with those of comparably experienced and educated civilians?; (2) Do military retirees enjoy higher relative wage growth over their second careers than their civilian peers?; and (3) Is the transition to civilian employment a difficult process for military retirees? This research can be viewed as in the same vein as recent research on immigrants that compares their earnings upon arrival in the United States and afterward to the earnings of native-born workers (for example, see Borjas, 1994).

As with the earlier research on military retirees, this study finds, using several data sets including the 1996 Survey of Retired Military Personnel (SRMP), that the relative civilian earnings of retirees in

---

[5]See Warner and Asch (1995) for a review of this literature.

[6]Estimates of the effect of military service on civilian earnings range anywhere between negative 35 percent for white Vietnam-era veterans (Angrist, 1989) to positive 5 percent for non-Hispanic whites in the post-Vietnam era (Gilroy et al., 1992).

1995 are substantially higher among those who separated in the 1970s than among those who separated in the 1990s. This study also found, however, that the relative earnings of retirees upon separation from the military have fallen with successive cohorts. Together, these two facts imply a low level of relative wage growth for retirees over the course of their civilian careers.

This conclusion contrasts with the findings of earlier research suggesting that military retirees who enter the civilian labor market with below-average wages tend to catch up with their civilian peers after five to ten years in the civilian labor market (Borjas and Welch, 1986; Cardell et al., 1997). This report attributes this difference in findings to the failure of earlier research to control for cohort effects, which can bias cross-sectional estimates of relative wage growth. Chapter Two presents these findings along with a general literature review. Chapter Two also explores the sensitivity of these main findings to alternative data and methodological assumptions.

Chapter Three argues that one should perhaps not be surprised that the wages of retirees do not catch up with those of civilians. First, by failing to control for the unobservable determinants of reenlistment, the study may be comparing retirees to an inappropriate civilian reference group. It may also be unreasonable to expect retirees, after they are in the civilian labor market, to develop a set of skills that catapults them beyond their initial civilian peers. Retirees may leave the military with such a well-established skill set that it is difficult for them to improve upon it.

Finally, one should also expect the high level of pension income that retirees receive to diminish the level of effort they are willing to expend once they enter the civilian labor market. More puzzling is the decline in relative retiree wages observed across cohorts; this report suggests several avenues for further research on this topic.

Chapter Three also presents evidence on the nature of the transition to civilian employment. Describing this transition is important because whereas the stated purpose of the pension system is largely to function as a force-management tool,[7] it is frequently argued that the

---

[7]See, for example, the Hook Commission Report of 1948 (U.S. Government Printing Office, 1948).

pension system also serves an important function in maintaining retirees' standard of living as they transition from military to civilian careers.

Using the SRMP, this report presents a variety of descriptive statistics derived from both quantitative and qualitative questions that seem to indicate that most retirees find the transition relatively painless. Retirees find civilian employment quickly and there is no evidence that they require an unusual level of training to accomplish those jobs. Perhaps most significant, retirees report being happy with their civilian life and few believe that their military service hampered the development of a satisfying civilian career. At a minimum, this suggests that the observed gap in earnings between retirees and civilians cannot be attributable to military service alone. Part of the gap in earnings must be attributable to unobserved differences between civilians and retirees, whether those differences are in terms of ability, effort, or the types of jobs and responsibilities military retirees select.

In the end, this research does not reveal whether the military has set its current annuity at an optimal level, but it does suggest that retirees, at least, find it to be an adequate benefit. On this point, Chapter Three presents evidence showing that total earnings (civilian wages plus retiree pay) of retirees is comparable to their prior military earnings and exceeds the mean earnings of their civilian peers. Whether the annuity is set too low in the sense that the military loses high-ability individuals early on to civilian careers or too high in the sense that it overcompensates retirees relative to their civilian opportunities is a more complicated question that must await further research.

Chapter Two

COMPARING CIVILIAN AND RETIREE WAGE GROWTH

This chapter first reviews the previous literature on the civilian earnings of military retirees, focusing on both the empirical estimates of retiree-civilian earnings differentials and the theoretical explanation for these observed differences. I also discuss the importance of controlling for cohort effects in estimating earnings differentials over time, a point made forcefully in related literature on immigrant earnings.

In this chapter, I establish, using the SRMP, that retiree and civilian wages grow at about the same rate and that over time retirees have entered the civilian labor force at increasingly low relative wages. I also explore how relative starting wages and wage growth vary with retiree characteristics. I validate these findings using several alternative data sources. Finally, I show that declining real wages in the lower half of the civilian wage distribution is partly responsible for the low rate of relative retiree wage growth.

PREVIOUS LITERATURE

Cooper (1981) and Borjas and Welch (1986) first studied the civilian earnings of military retirees using data from the 1977 Department of Defense Retiree Survey (DRS) and a sample of veterans from the 1977 March Current Population Survey (CPS). Using similar methodologies, both studies concluded that military retirees earn less than their civilian counterparts upon separation, but that military retiree earnings catch up as retirees gain civilian experience.[1] The civilian wages of military retirees grow faster than the wages of comparable civilians. Borjas and Welch (1986), for example, found that officers working full-time year-round (FTYR) earned 27 percent less than comparable civilians at age 44—soon after the officers enter the civilian labor force—but by age 65 this difference had declined to 4 percent. For FTYR enlisted personnel, the wage differential was greater than 30 percent upon separation at age 41, but about 5 percent at age 65.[2] Two more recent studies—Pleeter (1995) and Cardell et al. (1997)—come to similar conclusions using 1990 census data and the 1996 SRMP, respectively.

Borjas and Welch (1986) explain this pattern with a simple model of human capital accumulation in which military retirees lacking civilian labor market skills engage in an intensive period of "retooling" upon separation. This explains both their relatively low wages upon retirement and the convergence with civilian wages over time. Military training is not necessarily transferable to the civilian sector, a point emphasized in much of the literature on the postservice earnings of veterans.

Thus, it is natural to assume that military retirees will need additional training upon separation in order to compete in the civilian labor market. Convergence follows if one believes the marginal return to human capital accumulation for the average retiree is higher than that for the average civilian. This explanation seems plausible given that military retirees enter the civilian labor market after age 40. Most civilians by that age have entered long-term employment and have completed the bulk of whatever human capital investments they are going to make in their lifetime. Also, the comparatively low wages of retirees upon separation implies a comparatively low opportunity cost of human capital investment.[3]

---

[1]Both studies control for civilian experience, educational attainment, race, and region of residence.

[2]Cooper (1981) finds a lower initial gap and therefore an earlier age at which the earnings path of military retirees intersects that of civilians. In an earlier paper, Borjas and Welch (1983) argue, however, that Cooper's methodology systematically biases retiree earnings upward.

[3]An alternative explanation for convergence is the possibility that civilian employers are imperfectly informed about the match quality of retirees. Imperfect information of

A similar story emerges in the earliest papers written on the economic progress of immigrants in their host countries. Chiswick (1978), for example, found through using the 1970 census that immigrants at the time of their arrival to the United States earn 17 percent less than natives. Faster wage growth among immigrants, however, implies immigrant earnings overtake the earnings of native-born workers within 15 years of arrival, and within 30 years exceed native earnings by 11 percent. The immigration literature uses similar arguments to explain these observations; namely, upon arrival, immigrants have low levels of U.S.-specific skills (for example, English language proficiency), but as they accumulate these skills their human capital rises relative to natives and therefore the earnings of immigrant and native-born workers tend to converge.[4]

It was Borjas (1985) who first argued that the immigrant-native earnings comparisons in earlier research were potentially misleading due to the failure to control for cohort effects. (By *cohort,* I mean a group of individuals born at roughly the same point in time.) In a single cross-section (that is, a single year of data), such as the U.S. Census, the correlation between earnings and time-since-arrival could simply reflect differences among immigrants arriving in the United States at different times. In fact, there are good reasons to believe that the immigrants arriving in the United States in the 1960s and earlier came with skills more suitable to the U.S. economy of that time than those of immigrants arriving in the 1970s and later (LaLonde and Topel, 1990).

If one were to take a snapshot of immigrant earnings in 1980, it may appear that immigrant earnings grow relative to native earnings the more time an immigrant spends in the adoptive country, when in fact all that is being observed is a decrease in the ratio of immigrant-to-native earnings in succeeding cohorts of immigrants. The basic problem is that one cannot distinguish the effect on earnings of

---

this sort could cause employers to hire retirees at wages below true marginal productivity. Over time as match quality is revealed, retiree wages rise relative to the wages of civilians. Warner and Simon (1992) provide evidence for this hypothesis using data on civilian scientists and engineers.

[4]Borjas (1994) points out that the human capital hypothesis is not enough to explain why immigrant earnings overtake native earnings. He argues that this high relative wage growth among immigrants is most easily explained by positive selection; only the most hard-working and motivated individuals choose to immigrate.

time-since-arrival from the effect of being in a particular immigrant cohort in a cross-sectional analysis. As Borjas (1994, p. 1672) writes, ". . . we cannot use the current labor market experiences of those who arrived twenty years ago to forecast the earnings of newly arrived immigrants."

Research on the postservice earnings of military retirees suffers from the same sort of criticism. Cardell et al. (1997), for example, predicts substantial convergence in earnings using cross-sectional data on retirees age 37 to 64 in 1995. There is little reason to suppose, however, that the earnings of retirees age 37 in 1995 will converge with the earnings of retirees age 64 in 1995. The labor market experiences of the 64-year-olds may be a poor proxy for the experiences of the 37-year-olds who will not turn 64 until 2023. These individuals joined the military in very different eras and perhaps for very different reasons and their earnings relative to civilians will likely reflect those differences.

In the SRMP, for example, the average 37-year-old observed in 1995 joined the military in 1974 and retired in 1994. On the other hand, the average 64-year-old retiree observed in 1995 joined the military in 1951 and retired in 1971. Among other differences, the 64-year-old was much more likely to have entered the military via the draft than the 37-year-old. They also entered the civilian labor market in very different eras and therefore may have been presented with different civilian opportunities upon separation. Ironically, Borjas and Welch (1986) fail to acknowledge the potential importance of cohort effects when they predict, based a single cross-section of data for 1976, that retiree wages converge with the wages of comparable civilians as retirees gain civilian labor market experience. Cooper (1981) and Pleeter (1995) also neglect to account for cohort effects when interpreting the results of their own studies.

Borjas' observation in 1985 inspired attempts to track immigrant earnings longitudinally using both panel data sets on individuals (that is, data sets with repeated observations on the same individuals) and by creating synthetic cohorts of individuals in repeated cross-sections such as the decennial censuses. Use of longitudinal data controls for cohort effects by following specific cohorts over time. These longitudinal studies showed substantially less convergence in earnings among immigrants arriving post-1970 than among immigrants arriving prior to 1970. Indeed, Borjas (1994) argues it is unlikely that the earnings of more-recent immigrants will ever catch up with those of U.S. natives. The analysis of retiree earnings presented later in this chapter comes to a similar conclusion.

CONSTRUCTING THE ANALYSIS DATA SET

This report derives its main results from a comparison of retiree earnings recorded in the 1996 SRMP and civilian earnings recorded in various years of the March CPS. The SRMP surveyed 24,857 active duty personnel who retired between 1971 and 1994 with 20 or more years of creditable service. The sample excludes National Guard and Reserve retirees and retirees who resided outside the United States, took early retirement, or suffered from a severe disability. The sample includes roughly equal numbers of retirees from the 1971 to 1974, 1975 to 1979, 1980 to 1984, 1985 to 1989, and 1990 to 1994 retirement cohorts, and substantially overrepresents non-whites and officers. Whereas officers and non-whites constitute roughly 25 and 15 percent of the actual population of military retirees, respectively, they represent approximately 49 and 48 percent of the SRMP sample (Henry and Riemer, 1997). Marine Corps retirees were also oversampled, although to a much lesser degree than officers and non-whites.

The survey, conducted by mail by the Defense Manpower Data Center (DMDC) between March 1996 and July 1997, obtained 19,484 usable responses—a response rate of 80 percent. The CPS is a nationally representative survey of approximately 60,000 households conducted monthly. The March demographic supplement asks a wide range of questions including detailed questions on labor earnings in the past year.[5]

The SRMP asked respondents a wide range of questions concerning their separation from the military, experience in the civilian labor market, health and use of health services, use of military commissaries and exchanges, labor and non-labor income, spousal income,

---

[5]See Riemer and Lamoreaux (1997) and Henry and Riemer (1997) for a more detailed description of the SRMP survey instrument and sampling design. Also see http://www.bls.census.gov/cps for more on the CPS sampling design.

and basic demographics such as marital status and education. In addition, the DMDC matched administrative data from the Pension and Active Duty Military and Loss Edit Files that provide further details on items such as rank, military occupation, terms of separation, demographics, years of service, and pension income.

The SRMP collected earnings data for two points in time: (1) earnings on the first full-time job following retirement and (2) earnings in 1995.[6] This longitudinal feature of the SRMP is instrumental to this analysis. Because of the wide range of age cohorts sampled in the SRMP, these data allow the calculation of the rate of growth in retiree wages among a variety of ages and over a variety of time periods. For example, one might observe the wages of a retiree surveyed at age 60 in both 1995 and when the retiree separated at age 41 in 1976. Likewise, wages are observed for a 50-year-old who separated at age 42 in both 1988 and 1995. The ability to observe wages longitudinally in the SRMP allows one to control for cohort effects which could bias purely cross-sectional estimates.

I impose a number of sample restrictions on the SRMP and CPS data (see Table 2.1 for an itemized list of restrictions and their marginal effect on sample size). I restrict samples in both data sets to non-disabled males age 38 to 64 with a high-school degree or more working full time, earning more than one-half the minimum wage but less than CPS topcoded wages, and not self-employed.[7] I define full-time workers as those working more than four months per year and 35 hours per week. I further restrict the SRMP sample to those individuals retiring between ages 37 and 50 with at least 20 years of service (YOS) and with rank E-5 to E-9, W-2 to W-4, or O-3 to O-6. After imposing sample restrictions and eliminating observations with missing data, I am left with 5,281 retirees and an average of approximately 7,200 observations per year in the CPS.

These restrictions are intended to eliminate outliers as well as focus the analysis on individuals with relatively strong attachment to the labor force. Also, the question on year of retirement earnings in the SRMP is for the respondent's first full-time job.

---

[6]I take up the issue of recall bias later in this chapter.

[7]I use the minimum wage in 1991 of $4.25 an hour.

Table 2.1

SRMP Sample Restrictions

Sample Restriction	Sample Size
Base sample	24,993
Eligible, non-disabled males	18,449
Positive earnings	11,688
Work > 35 hours/week, 16 weeks/year	8,321
Earn more than minimum wage and less than CPS topcoded wages	7,446
Age 38–64	7,338
High school or more	6,573
Not self-employed	6,569
Retired age 37–50	6,224
Rank E-5–E-9, W-2–W-4, O-3–O-6	6,207
No missing data	5,281

The largest reduction in the SRMP sample size comes from restricting the sample to retirees who worked full time in both their year of retirement and 1995. I impose this restriction so that the same set of retirees is observed in both years. Of the 18,449 non-disabled males in the SRMP, 11,688 reported positive earnings in both the year of retirement and 1995—63 percent of the eligible sample. By comparison, restricting the CPS sample to males with positive earnings leaves 78 percent of the original sample.

The comparatively large drop in sample size in the SRMP is due to a relatively high level of non-response to the earnings question and the restriction that SRMP respondents have positive earnings in both 1995 and year of retirement. The fact that hours and weeks worked conditional on full-time employment are equivalent in the SRMP and CPS in both 1995 and year of retirement, and unconditional hours and weeks worked are also equivalent in 1995, diminishes concern that this sample restriction seriously biases the results presented in the following sections. Age-specific 1995 employment hazards in the SRMP and CPS are also comparable.

POOLED REGRESSION ANALYSIS

Consider the following log wage equation in which retiree and civilian data are pooled in a given year, 1995:

$$\ln y_i = \beta_{95}^T X_i + AGE_i \alpha_{95} + MR_i \delta_{95} + \phi_{95}^T AGE_i \cdot MR_i + \varepsilon_i \qquad (1)$$

where y_i is the monthly wage of individual i, AGE_i represents a full set of age dummies, $MR_i = 1$ if the individual is a military retiree and equals zero otherwise, and X_i is a vector of standard demographic covariates. The sum of the coefficient vector $[\hat{\delta}_{95} + \hat{\phi}_{95}^T]$ provides estimates of the differences in wages between retirees and civilians at given ages.

I first estimate Equation 1 using data on 1995 wages in the SRMP and 1995 wages for civilians taken from the 1996 March CPS. In addition to age and retiree status, I am able to control for a number of individual characteristics, including education (four categories), race (black/white), marital status (married/not married), occupation (nine categories), employer type (private/public), and region (four categories). Table 2.2 presents the means of these covariates and the dependent variable (monthly wages) by retiree/civilian status.[8]

Civilian monthly wages are about 23 percent higher than retiree monthly wages in 1995. This is despite the fact that retirees are somewhat older, more educated, and more likely to be employed in professional occupations. On the other hand, the retiree sample has a disproportionate number of blacks and individuals who reside in the South which could account for part of the gap between retiree and civilian wages. In any case, the substantial differences in the observable characteristics of civilians and retirees that are evident in Table 2.2 suggest wage comparisons should be conditional on these characteristics.

In Figure 2.1, the vector $[\hat{\delta}_{95} + \hat{\phi}_{95}^T]$ is graphed from estimating Equation 1 by ordinary least squares (OLS) (full regression results are reported in Table 2.3). Retiree wages at age 38 appear to be substantially lower (about 37 percent less) than comparable civilian wages at that age. This initial gap then diminishes steadily with age. For most ages after age 56, the difference between retiree and civilian monthly wages is insignificantly different from zero at conventional

---

[8]I chose monthly wages because hourly and weekly wages cannot be constructed in the SRMP for earnings upon separation.

Table 2.2

1995 Sample Means, by Retiree Status

Variable	Retiree	Civilian
1995 monthly wage	$2,958	$3,829
Age	51	47
Black	0.303	0.063
Married	0.874	0.792
Educational attainment		
High school	0.147	0.353
Some college	0.372	0.287
College degree	0.185	0.213
> College degree	0.297	0.148
Civilian occupation		
Manager	0.328	0.210
Professional	0.284	0.188
Clerical	0.085	0.057
Sales	0.060	0.115
Craft	0.096	0.022
Operator/transport	0.045	0.243
Laborer	0.090	0.064
Service	0.090	0.071
Agriculture	0.003	0.029
Private sector	0.631	0.811
Region		
East	0.059	0.218
Midwest	0.103	0.255
South	0.570	0.284
West	0.268	0.244
N	5,281	11,384

NOTES: See text for sample restriction. N = number of observations.
SOURCES: 1996 SRMP and 1996 CPS.

levels. This essentially replicates the findings of Cardell et al. (1997) and is very similar in spirit to the results of earlier research on military retirees; the civilian wages of military retirees appear to converge with civilian wages as retirees gain increased civilian experience.

With a single cross-section, as in Equation 1, one cannot distinguish between age and cohort effects because age in 1995 is strongly correlated with year of separation. This problem with the cross-sectional estimation of wage convergence is evident if one were to run a similar regression except with data on wages in year of retirement.

$$\ln y_{it} = \beta_s^T X_{it} + YEAR_{it}\alpha_s + MR_{it}\delta_s + \phi_s^T YEAR_{it} \cdot MR_{it} + v_{it} \qquad (2)$$

where y_{it} now represents civilian monthly wages in year t (1995 dollars), $YEAR_{it}$ is a full set of year dummies corresponding to the year of separation in the retiree sample, and X_{it} now contains age, but not region of residence.[9] The sum $[\hat{\delta}_s + \hat{\phi}_s^T]$ reveals how the difference between retiree and civilian wages at the time of separation varies across cohorts.[10]

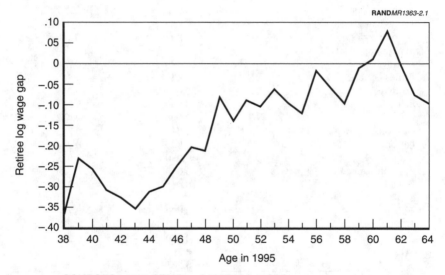

SOURCES: 1996 SRMP and 1996 March CPS.

Figure 2.1—Retiree Log Wage Gap in 1995, by Age

---

[9]I discount earnings using the CPI-U-X1 series. Following Boskin et al. (1998), I reduce the implied rate of inflation in the series by 1 percent annually. Region of residence upon retirement is not available in the SRMP.

[10]SRMP earnings are for the first full-time job held following separation. Strictly speaking, then, these earnings are not necessarily measured in the retirees' year of retirement. More than 75 percent of the retirees in the SRMP sample, however, entered a full-time job within 12 months of retirement.

Table 2.3

The Effect of Retiree Status and Age on 1995 Wages

Variable	Coefficient	Standard Error
Educational attainment		
High school	−0.481	0.015
Some college	−0.366	0.013
College degree	−0.217	0.014
Married	0.166	0.011
Black	−0.052	0.013
Occupation		
Manager	0.582	0.031
Professional	0.485	0.032
Clerical	0.251	0.034
Sales	0.322	0.032
Craft	0.189	0.036
Operator/transport	0.286	0.031
Laborer	0.206	0.035
Service	0.109	0.033
Region	0.037	0.011
East	0.054	0.013
Midwest	0.027	0.013
South	−0.033	0.011
Retiree	−0.095	0.104
Retiree × Age		
38	−0.272	0.151
39	−0.137	0.130
40	−0.158	0.125
41	−0.213	0.118
42	−0.228	0.117
43	−0.256	0.115
44	−0.217	0.113
45	−0.204	0.111
46	−0.153	0.112
47	−0.110	0.110
48	−0.118	0.112
49	0.010	0.113
50	−0.044	0.112
51	0.005	0.111
52	−0.008	0.112
53	0.031	0.113
54	−0.002	0.112
55	−0.024	0.114
56	0.076	0.114
57	0.039	0.115
58	0.000	0.116

Table 2.3 (continued)

Variable	Coefficient	Standard Error
59	0.084	0.116
60	0.104	0.119
61	0.170	0.121
62	0.095	0.127
63	0.019	0.135

NOTES: Regression includes controls for age. Excluded categories include > college degree, agricultural occupation, residence in the West, and age 64.

SOURCES: 1996 SRMP and 1996 March CPS.

A graph of $[\hat{\delta}_s + \hat{\phi}_s^T]$ by year (see Figure 2.2) reveals that retirees who separated in the early 1970s earned wages comparable to, if not more than, those of civilians upon separation but that more-recent retirees earned substantially less. Consequently, over time, the wages earned by retirees when they first leave the military have declined substantially relative to civilian wages. These strong cohort effects imply that the age-earnings profile represented in Figure 2.1 is misleading. Figure 2.3 emphasizes this point by graphing $[\hat{\delta}_{95} + \hat{\phi}_{95}^T]$ and $[\hat{\delta}_s + \hat{\phi}_s^T]$ together.[11]

The solid line in Figure 2.3 represents relative 1995 wages of retirees by their age in 1995. Closely tracking this line is the dashed line representing relative wages of those same retirees in their first full-time job following retirement.

The implication of Figure 2.3 is that the relative wages of any given military retiree is roughly constant over the retiree's second career, implying little or no convergence in wages. A retiree age 50 in 1995, for example, earned 15 percent less in his first full-time job than a comparable civilian; but, this same individual was earning 16 percent less than a comparable civilian in 1995 as well. Although not illustrated in the figure, the average 50-year-old retiree in 1995 had been retired for nine years. In contrast, an individual age 62 earned wages about 2 percent lower than those of his civilian peers in 1995.

_____

[11]These estimates do not control for region of residence because this variable is not available for year of retirement in the SRMP. This could affect the estimated wage gap because retirees are more concentrated in the South where wages are lower. Including 1995 region of residence in the year-of-retirement regression did not affect the results, however.

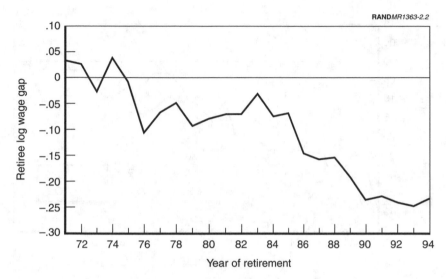

SOURCES: 1996 SRMP and 1972 to 1995 March CPS.

Figure 2.2—Retiree Log Wage Gap in Year of Retirement

The retiree entered the civilian labor market 20 years earlier with wages comparable to those of his peers.

Table 2.4 summarizes Figure 2.3 by estimating Equation 1 and Equation 2 separately by retiree cohort: 1971 to 1974, 1975 to 1979, 1980 to 1984, 1985 to 1989, and 1990 to 1994. The column labeled YOR (for Year of Retirement) under the All Retirees column reports the relative log wages of all retirees in their first full-time civilian job and the column labeled 1995 under All Retirees reports relative log wages in 1995.

This cohort-specific analysis shows little evidence of the kind of wage convergence implied by the simple cross-sectional estimates in Figure 2.1. Relative wages improve slightly for older cohorts of retirees and remain essentially unchanged for more-recent cohorts. Individuals separating in 1975 to 1979, for example, earned about 7 percent less than their civilian peers in their first full-time civilian job. By 1995, that difference had declined to 2 percent. For individuals retiring between 1985 and 1989, the log wage gap held steady—

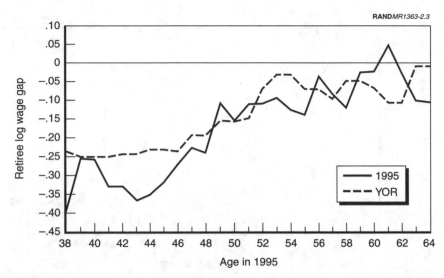

RAND*MR1363-2.3*

NOTE: YOR series consists of $(\delta_s + \phi_s)$ from Figure 2.2 corresponding to the average year of retirement associated with each age in 1995.

SOURCES: 1996 SRMP and 1972 to 1996 March CPS.

Figure 2.3— Retiree Log Wage Gap in 1995 and Year of Retirement, by Age

from 12 to 14 percent between year of retirement and 1995. The most-recent retirees (1990 to 1994) saw their relative wages decline by about 7 percentage points between year of retirement and 1995. Of course, it is important to note that neither the experience of the 1970 to 1974 cohort nor the experience of more-recent cohorts is necessarily a good barometer for what will happen to the relative wages of the 1990 to 1994 retirees in the future.

Table 2.4 also presents estimates of the log wage gap for enlistees and officers separately. In general, the relative wages of enlistees in the year of retirement are less than those of officers. For example, enlisted personnel retiring in 1980 to 1984 earned 11 percent less than comparable civilians whereas officers earned 2 percent more. These differences beg the question whether enlisted personnel leave the military with skills less amenable to civilian employment than those of officers. In fact, enlisted personnel are substantially more likely to report a low level of skill transferability than are officers, especially among more-recent cohorts (see Chapter Three).

Table 2.4

Log Wage Gap in Year of Retirement and 1995, by Retiree Cohort and Rank

Retiree Cohort	All Retirees		Enlisted Personnel		Officers	
	YOR	1995	YOR	1995	YOR	1995
1971–74	0.007	0.080	0.027	0.084	−0.090	0.108
	(0.026)	(0.037)	(0.031)	(0.043)	(0.024)	(0.069)
1975–79	−0.071	−0.020	−0.071	0.009	−0.043	−0.082
	(0.014)	(0.024)	(0.019)	(0.030)	(0.050)	(0.037)
1980–84	−0.044	−0.048	−0.112	−0.017	0.020	−0.085
	(0.013)	(0.019)	(0.018)	(0.027)	(0.019)	(0.027)
1985–89	−0.123	−0.135	−0.221	−0.175	−0.054	−0.129
	(0.013)	(0.017)	(0.020)	(0.025)	(0.018)	(0.024)
1990–94	−0.248	−0.315	−0.365	−0.368	−0.181	−0.303
	(0.012)	(0.017)	(0.020)	(0.025)	(0.017)	(0.023)

NOTES: Log wage gap represents coefficient on retiree dummy in regression of log monthly wages on age, education, race, marital status, occupation, and private/public employment. Regressions are estimated separately by retiree cohort.
SOURCES: 1996 SRMP and 1972 to 1996 March CPS.

Curiously, whereas officers fare better than enlisted personnel in the year of retirement relative to civilians, their wages tend to fall relative to civilian wages over time. Again looking at the 1980 to 1984 cohort, officers enter the civilian labor market earning wages 2 percent above those of civilians, but by 1995 their wages are 9 percent below the wages of civilians. The relative wages of enlisted personnel, on the other hand, seem to improve slightly.

One can test more systematically for differences in relative wages and relative growth rates among different groups of retirees by creating individual-level observations on relative wages and relative wage growth, as follows in Equations 3 and 4,

$$\Omega_i = \left\{ \left[\frac{y^r_{ix_i,95} - y^r_{ix_i,s}}{y^r_{ix_i,s}} \right] - \left[\frac{\bar{y}^c_{x_i,95} - \bar{y}^c_{x_i,s}}{\bar{y}^c_{x_i,s}} \right] \right\} \frac{1}{s} \tag{3}$$

$$\Delta_i = \ln y^r_{ix_i,s} - \ln \bar{y}^c_{x_i,s} \tag{4}$$

where the first term in Equation 3 is the wage growth of retiree i between 1995 and year of separation, s, with the set of characteristics x_i and the second term is wage growth for a comparable civilian. The second term in Equation 3 is calculated by taking the mean of the wages of individuals in the CPS with the same set of characteristics as the retiree. In effect, this involves creating synthetic cohorts of individuals within the CPS as a proxy for true longitudinal data on civilians. A value of $\Omega_i < 0$ for a given retiree implies his wages grew more slowly than civilian wages between retirement and 1995 and a value of $\Omega_i > 0$ implies his wages grew more rapidly than civilian wages. In other words, a negative value of Ω_i means that the retiree's wages fell relative to civilian wages between retirement and 1995, while a positive value of Ω_i indicates his wages increased relative to civilian wages.

To achieve sufficient cell sizes in the CPS sample, I reduced the number of covariates in x_i by limiting the age categories to two-year intervals, reducing the occupational categories to white versus blue collar, reducing the educational categories to high school, some college, and college and above, and eliminating region altogether.

The term Δ_i (see Equation 4) is simply the difference in log wages upon separation between retirees and comparable civilians.[12] A negative value of Δ_i, for example, tells that a given retiree earned wages below what a comparable civilian earned in his year of retirement. The means of Δ_i and Ω_i (see Table 2.5) are consistent with the results of Table 2.4.

Table 2.6 reports the results of the following linear regressions aimed at highlighting how Δ_i and Ω_i vary across retirees with varying characteristics:

---

[12]Because the CPS data do not follow specific individuals over time, it is not possible to make a precise mapping of CPS growth rates to SRMP growth rates. In the SRMP, the characteristics of individuals change between year of retirement and 1995. I experiment with several mappings including matching CPS wages to the SRMP retirees using both retiree characteristics in their year of retirement and in 1995 (see Panel B in Table 2.5) and matching CPS wages on the basis of year of retirement characteristics only (see Panel A in Table 2.5). Neither mapping is entirely satisfactory, but they are the best that can be done without a comparable longitudinal survey of civilians.

$$\Omega_i = X_i\beta + R_i\alpha + \varepsilon_i \tag{5}$$

$$\Delta_i = X_i\delta + R_i\gamma + v_i \tag{6}$$

where R_i contains characteristics of retirees, such as year of retirement, civilian experience, rank, tenure, and military and civilian occupation. I also include a variable indicating whether an individual obtained additional education following separation.

A number of interesting results emerge from the regression coefficients reported in Table 2.6. Consistent with results reported in Table 2.4, the coefficient estimates of the Δ_i regression (the left column under Dependent Variable in Table 2.6) indicate that enlisted individuals fare substantially worse than warrant and commissioned officers in their first full-time jobs $(\hat{\delta}_{Enlisted} = -0.212)$. The results also indicate that individuals who report a high level of transferability between their military and civilian occupations fare better relative to their civilian peers than those who do not.

Table 2.5

Retiree-Civilian Difference in Log Wages and Growth Rates,
by Retiree Cohort

Retiree Cohort	Δ	Ω
A. Match YOR only		
1971–74	−0.075	−0.004
1975–79	−0.143	−0.0003
1980–84	−0.115	−0.014
1985–89	−0.247	−0.003
1990–94	−0.339	−0.081
B. Match 1995 and YOR		
1971–74	−0.075	0.005
1975–79	−0.143	0.005
1980–84	−0.115	−0.010
1985–89	−0.247	−0.005
1990–94	−0.339	−0.062

NOTES: In Panel A, CPS wages are matched to SRMP retirees based on YOR characteristics only. In Panel B, CPS wages are matched to SRMP retirees based on both YOR and 1995 characteristics.
SOURCES: 1996 SRMP and 1972 to 1996 March CPS.

Table 2.6

The Effect of Retiree Characteristics on Relative Wages and Wage Growth

	Dependent Variable	
	Δ	Ω
Education		
High school	0.093	−0.010
	(0.029)	(0.019)
Some college	0.023	−0.003
	(0.022)	(0.013)
Change in education	—	0.002
		(0.011)
Rank		
Enlisted	−0.212	0.009
	(0.023)	(0.014)
Warrant officer	−0.103	0.032
	(0.027)	(0.016)
Married	−0.133	0.000
	(0.026)	(0.015)
Black	0.170	−0.064
	(0.015)	(0.010)
Region		
East	0.066	−0.007
	(0.029)	(0.017)
Midwest	−0.030	−0.004
	(0.024)	(0.014)
South	−0.038	0.003
	(0.015)	(0.009)
White collar	0.069	−0.082
	(0.016)	(0.010)
Public	−0.064	−0.045
	(0.015)	(0.009)
Tenure	—	0.002
		(0.001)
Years in grade	−0.018	−0.011
	(0.003)	(0.008)
Transferable	0.151	0.003
	(0.014)	(0.002)
Service		
Army	−0.008	0.013
	(0.016)	(0.009)
Navy	0.054	−0.006
	(0.019)	(0.011)

Table 2.6 (continued)

	Dependent Variable	
	Δ	Ω
Marines	−0.010	−0.007
	(0.028)	(0.016)
R^2	0.146	0.062

NOTES: Both regressions include controls for year of separation and age at separation. Excluded categories include College, Officers, the West region, and the Air Force.
SOURCES: 1996 SRMP and 1972 to 1996 March CPS.

This result on transferability is consistent with a regression of Δ_i on military occupation (not shown in Table 2.6). Individuals in military occupations such as engineering, electronics, intelligence, and health care all fare better relative to civilians than do individuals who worked in occupations that one might think would develop less transferable skills (for example, combat arms). Navy personnel and those who remained in their last grade for fewer years also fared better.

The estimated coefficients on High school, Married, Black, White collar, and Public listed in the Δ column in Table 2.6 are also of interest. The coefficient of 0.093 on High school, for example, indicates that retirees with a high-school level education fare better relative to their reference group than do college graduates (the excluded category). Similarly, the coefficient of 0.170 on Black in this regression suggests black retirees fare better relative to their reference group than do white retirees, conditional on other individual characteristics such as education.

These results may indicate that military service serves as a relatively strong positive signal to civilian employers for minorities and less-educated individuals. Other results in the Δ column in Table 2.6 indicate that being unmarried, living in the Northeast, being a professional, or working in the public sector positively influence relative retiree wages in the first full-time job.

Turning now to the Ω_i regression (the right-hand column in Table 2.6), relative growth in wages was stronger among retirees who had high tenure in their 1995 job. Interacting tenure with retiree cohort reveals, though, that tenure has a positive effect on relative wage growth only among the most-recent retirees. This suggests that job churning depresses wage growth at first, but over the long run may have positive effects on relative wages. Few other covariates have a statistically significant effect on relative wage growth. Whereas blacks have comparatively high relative wages in their first job, their relative wage growth is substantially less than that of whites. Professionals and individuals working in the private sector also experience low relative wage growth. Curiously, individuals who pursued more education following separation (about 16 percent of the sample) did not experience higher wage growth than those who did not. Military occupation (not shown in Table 2.6) had little effect on relative wage growth.

ADDRESSING THE PROBLEM OF BIASED REPORTS ON EARNINGS

One of the more striking features of Table 2.4 is the strong downward trend in the relative earnings of retirees by year of retirement. The oldest cohort of retirees fared much better in their first full-time job relative to civilians than did the youngest cohort. This trend cannot be explained by observable factors such as occupational choice. Before considering potential explanations for a downward trend in relative retiree earnings, however, it is worth considering whether sample selection or the way in which the SRMP data were collected might be contributing to this apparent trend.

I lose nearly a quarter of the SRMP sample by imposing the restriction that respondents report positive earnings in both their initial full-time job and in 1995. This could account for the apparent downward trend in relative retiree earnings if the sample of individuals with missing data actually have lower earnings than the sample with complete data and if this difference is larger in older cohorts. That is, the problem of sample selection could be more severe in older cohorts.

To the extent this selection is based on unobservable characteristics, little can be done to document it. On observable characteristics, however, the samples with missing and non-missing earnings data look quite similar. For example, the distribution of rank is the same across samples. The proportion of the missing and non-missing samples reporting having comparable or better wages than their civilian peers, and the proportion who report military service diminished their ability to earn a fair civilian wage, are also the same. On observable grounds, at least, it does not appear that sample selection is driving the results shown in Table 2.4.

A weakness of the SRMP is that it relies on respondents to recall their earnings from their first full-time job following military retirement. For individuals separating in the early 1970s this requires recalling what they earned up to 25 years ago. This is a significant amount of time and one should be concerned about the ability of older retirees to make accurate estimates of these past earnings. By comparison, data on civilian earnings in the CPS come from reports of earnings in the last calendar year.

Of particular concern is the possibility that retirees systematically bias their estimates of distant earnings in one direction or the other.[13] Suppose that retirees tend to overestimate distant earnings. This might happen if individuals tend to recall past earnings in survey-year dollars, perhaps because they think of past earnings relative to their earnings today. Regardless of the reason, a large upward bias in past earnings estimates could account for the strong negative trend in relative retiree earnings observed in Table 2.4 as well as the failure to find evidence that the relative wages of individual retirees improves with civilian labor market experience. Of course, retirees could also underestimate past earnings, in which case the true decline in relative retiree earnings is even more severe than what is reported in Table 2.4.

A number of studies have attempted to assess the extent of measurement error in longitudinal earnings data. These studies generally emphasize that while the extent of measurement error is small, the nature of the measurement error violates the classical errors-in-variables model which assumes the error is uncorrelated with the explanatory variables and, in the case of panel data, over time. Studies comparing earnings data reported in the CPS and Panel Study of Income Dynamics (PSID) to "true" earnings data obtained from other sources have found that measurement error (the difference

---

[13]Random measurement error in earnings is of less concern because it does not, at least asymptotically, lead to a biased estimate of $[\hat{\delta}_s + \hat{\phi}_s]$, but only diminishes its precision.

between true and reported earnings) is negatively correlated with true earnings (Bound and Krueger, 1991; Bound et al., 1989; Pischke, 1995; Bollinger, 1998).[14] Of particular importance to this study is Bollinger's (1998) finding that this negative correlation between error and true earnings is driven largely by overreporting of earnings among low earners.

In an attempt to verify the accuracy of the SRMP earnings data, I explored four alternative sources of earnings data on military retirees. The first is the 1977 DRS used by Cooper (1981) and Borjas and Welch (1986). The 1977 DRS has a similar structure to the SRMP that asks retirees to report civilian earnings immediately following separation and in 1976. In Table 2.7, I report mean monthly earnings on the first full-time job following separation for respondents in both the 1977 DRS and 1996 SRMP who retired between 1971 and 1975. As can be seen in the table, enlistees in the 1977 DRS on average report earnings in their first full-time job that are almost 40 percent lower than those reported by enlistees who separated in the same years but were surveyed by the 1996 SRMP. For officers the gap is much less, but still substantial (about 12 percent). This gap persists at all points of the earnings distribution, although it appears to be most significant between the 50th and 75th percentiles.

Several issues exist in making comparisons between DRS and SRMP earnings reports, however. First, the SRMP asks for total earnings in the first 12 months of the respondent's first full-time job following separation. The DRS, on the other hand, asks respondents to report monthly earnings in the first full-time job with no restriction on the time period analyzed. If DRS respondents reported earnings in the first month of the first full-time job, it is possible that SRMP respondents would end up reporting higher average monthly earnings because of tenure effects. Selection bias may affect the comparison

---

[14]In the CPS validation study (Bollinger, 1998), reported earnings are compared with Social Security earnings. In the PSID validation study (Pischke, 1995), earnings reported from a sample of employees in a single large firm are compared with earnings reported by the employer. The PSID is a longitudinal survey of earnings beginning with a large sample of individuals in 1968.

Table 2.7

Monthly Wages in First Full-Time Job Following Retirement, by Rank and Year Reported ($)

	Enlisted Personnel		Officers	
	1977 DRS	1996 SRMP	1977 DRS	1996 SRMP
Mean	783	1,283	1,401	1,600
Percentile				
10th	400	500	600	650
25th	544	667	800	917
50th	655	1,000	1,150	1,333
75th	900	1,417	1,540	2,000
90th	1,139	2,375	2,333	2,917
N	150	699	128	798

NOTES: Sample is restricted as follows: male, active duty, voluntary, non-disability, age at retirement > 36, 1970 < YOR < 1976, YOS > 19, report working full time immediately following retirement, >dropout, not self-employed, 136 < monthly wages < 10,000. N = number of observations.

SOURCES: 1977 DRS and 1996 SRMP.

between DRS and SRMP earnings as well if SRMP respondents are healthier on average than DRS respondents by virtue of the fact that they are still alive and willing to participate in the survey 20 years later.

With the DRS, one can only verify earnings reports for retirees separating in the early 1970s. The only other direct evidence I have on the initial earnings of retirees comes from a special record of Social Security earnings of enlisted Army personnel separating between 1993 and 1995.[15] The data include up to six years of civilian earnings data on 19,393 Army enlistees who separated with 20 or more years of service.[16]

Table 2.8 lists mean annual civilian Social Security earnings by year of retirement. For those separating in 1993, the mean Social Security earnings of $16,612 in 1994 (their first full year in the civilian labor

---

[15]Social Security earnings data were also collected in 1982 on a large sample of veterans, including retirees, who separated between 1972 and 1980. This sample was known as the Post Service Earnings History File (PSEHF). The DMDC informed us that these data have since been lost.

[16]As is typical with Social Security data, earnings are reported as group means to protect confidentiality. Thus, the figures in Table 2.11 represent weighted means across groups.

Table 2.8

**Annual Social Security Earnings of Army Enlistees Retiring
in 1993 to 1995 ($)**

Earnings in	Year of Retirement		
	1993	1994	1995
1992	38,447	37,788	36,040
1993	20,545	38,519	36,723
1994	16,612	20,884	37,064
1995	19,838	17,946	21,092
1996	21,307	20,586	18,850
1997	23,142	22,600	22,323

SOURCE: Army Social Security Data File.

market following retirement) are close to the mean annual earnings
of $15,107 in the first full-time job reported by Army enlistees
surveyed in the SRMP who also separated in 1993. The 1995 Social
Security earnings of Army enlistees separating in 1994 are also close
to those reported in the SRMP ($17,946 versus $15,070).[17] Thus, year
of retirement earnings reported in the SRMP for the most-recent
retirees do not appear to be seriously biased.

Another source of data on the civilian earnings of military retirees is
the CPS itself. In addition to reporting veteran status of respondents,
the CPS indicates in the years 1976 and later whether a respondent is
currently receiving military retirement income. Prior to 1976, the CPS
indicates whether a respondent is receiving pension income from a
government employee pension. Unfortunately, the CPS does not report when a respondent last served in the military or his years of service. One can therefore identify the civilian wages of military retirees
in the CPS, but not when in their civilian careers those wages are
being earned. Consequently, an analysis comparable to that shown
in Table 2.4 is not possible with the CPS.

---

[17]Note that the SRMP and Social Security estimates may not be directly comparable
because Social Security data is not conditional on full-time employment nor does it
necessarily cover earnings in the retiree's first civilian job. The SRMP year of
retirement earnings data is for the first 12 months of the retiree's first full-time job.
How these discrepancies affect the comparison is unclear.

Table 2.9

Log Wage Gap in Year of Retirement and 1995: Alternative Retiree Samples

Retiree Cohort/	1995		YOR	
Age	SRMP/CPS	CPS-alone	SRMP/CPS	CPS-alone
1971–74/	−0.058	−0.086	−0.062	−0.224
58–64	(0.026)	(0.065)	(0.017)	(0.034)
1975–79/	−0.089	−0.147	−0.087	−0.238
53–57	(0.022)	(0.055)	(0.013)	(0.023)
1980–84/	−0.181	−0.231	−0.055	−0.203
48–52	(0.020)	(0.061)	(0.014)	(0.024)
1985–89/	−0.307	−0.214	−0.156	−0.249
43–47	(0.019)	(0.059)	(0.014)	(0.032)
1990–94/	−0.312	−0.316	−0.283	−0.300
38–42	(0.029)	(0.085)	(0.014)	(0.035)

NOTES: Log wage gap represents coefficient on retiree dummy in regression of log monthly wages on age, education, race, marital status, occupation, and private/public employment. Regressions are estimated separately by retiree cohort. YOR samples are restricted to individuals age 38 to 45 in year of retirement. 1995 CPS-alone sample employs 1994 and 1995 data.
SOURCES: 1996 SRMP and 1972 to 1996 March CPS.

A consistency check can, however, be performed on relative retiree earnings using the SRMP/CPS and CPS-alone samples. Table 2.9 reports the results of such an analysis.[18] In the two columns under 1995, I report the 1995 log wage gap by age. These results suggest that in 1995, at least, SRMP respondents reported civilian earnings in line with those of the CPS retiree sample. Only for retirees age 43 to 47 in 1995 do the log wage gap estimates diverge significantly (−0.307 versus −0.214) between the SRMP/CPS and CPS-alone samples.

Looking now at the two columns under YOR in Table 2.9, estimates of the log wage gap in the year of retirement do diverge significantly. I restrict the sample here to individuals age 38 to 45 in hopes that the CPS-alone retiree sample will be composed mostly of recent retirees.[19] Whereas the earnings for SRMP retirees are for their first

[18]The reader should note that the samples in Tables 2.4 and 2.9 are not directly comparable. The retiree sample in Table 2.4 is restricted according to rank and age at separation. This is not done in Table 2.9 because this information is not available for retirees in the CPS.

[19]I assume veterans receiving government pension income between 1971 and 1975 are retirees.

full-time job after separation, many of the CPS retirees will have been in the civilian labor force for several years. The differences in the estimated log wage gaps in the two samples are striking. In the 1971 to 1974 cohort, the log wage gap is –0.062 based on the SRMP sample and –0.224 in the CPS-alone sample. This difference in estimated wage gaps persists through the 1980 to 1984 cohort. The estimated wage gaps are somewhat closer in the 1985 to 1989 cohort and are essentially the same in the 1990 to 1994 cohort.

The retiree earnings data from the DRS and CPS, then, seem to indicate that the oldest retirees in the SRMP overestimated year of retirement earnings by a substantial amount. Unfortunately, neither data set alone allows me to conduct a panel analysis of wage growth as with SRMP data. For purposes of comparison, then, I finally turn to data from the U.S. Census which allows me to create a synthetic panel of retirees. In each census year, respondents were queried about their current military status and whether they had served over one or more periods including 1950 to 1955 (Korean War), 1955 to 1964, 1964 to 1975 (Vietnam War), 1975 to 1980, and 1980 to 1990.

Combining data on current age and dates of military service, I am able to identify military retirees in the census who separated in the years surrounding 1970, 1980, and 1990 (see the Appendix for the precise derivation of the retiree status variable). The mapping is not perfect and the sample likely contains veterans who are not in fact retirees (that is, they have served less than 20 years). Without years of service (available only in the 1990 census), though, it is not possible to identify retirees with total certainty.

With the census data, I create a synthetic panel of retirees across three census years with which to compare a similarly constructed synthetic panel of civilians. The idea behind a synthetic panel is to be able to track a cohort of individuals over time. For example, I assume that the 40- to 44-year-olds in the 1970 census are the same individuals in a statistical sense as the 50- to 54-year-olds in the 1980 census and the 60- to 64-year-olds in the 1990 census. It is not a true panel, however, because the same individuals are not surveyed in each year. I impose the same sample restrictions on the census data in terms of labor supply and other characteristics as I impose on the SRMP/CPS data.

Table 2.10 reports the coefficients on retiree status in a linear regression of log weekly and annual wages on retiree status and covariates (age, race, marital status, number of children in residence, education, census region, and employment sector) using a sample of males age 40 to 44 in 1970, 50 to 54 in 1980, and 60 to 64 in 1990. The coefficient on retiree status reveals how retiree wages compare in percentage terms to the wages of comparable civilians.

The first item of note in Table 2.10 is that relative earnings of retirees in the 1970 census (Panel A in the table) are far below those estimated for the 1971 to 1974 SRMP cohort. According to the census estimates, these retirees earn weekly wages 12 percent below those of comparable civilians when they first enter the civilian labor market. In contrast, the 1971 to 1974 SRMP cohort earned wages 15 percent higher than comparable civilians. The initial relative earnings of

Table 2.10

Coefficient on Retiree Indicator for Cohorts of Individuals Observed in the 1970, 1980, and 1990 Census

Sample/ Dependent Variable	Census Year		
	1970	1980	1990
A. Age 40–44 in 1970 (retired 1965–69)			
In weekly wages	−0.120	−0.172	−0.100
	(0.018)	(0.016)	(0.029)
In annual wages	−0.145	−0.174	−0.102
	(0.019)	(0.017)	(0.030)
B. Age 40–44 in 1980 (retired 1975–79)			
In weekly wages	—	−0.216	−0.123
		(0.021)	(0.025)
In annual wages	—	−0.253	−0.122
		(0.021)	(0.026)
C. Age 40–44 in 1990 (retired 1980–90)			
In weekly wages	—	—	−0.219
			(0.023)
In annual wages	—	—	−0.235
			(0.024)

NOTES: See text for sample restrictions and the Appendix for the definition of *retiree*. Regression coefficients are conditional on the following controls: age, race, marital status, number of children in residence, education, census region, and employment sector.

SOURCES: 1970, 1980, and 1990 Public Use Micro Sample.

retirees separating around 1980 (Panel B) are also much lower than wages estimated using the SRMP/CPS data. The weekly earnings of the 1980 census retirees fall about 22 percent below those of comparable civilians. The SRMP/CPS data for the 1980 to 1984 cohort showed no difference in the wages of retirees and civilians in the year of retirement. The census data therefore provide additional evidence that older retirees in the SRMP overestimated their YOR earnings. The relative wages of the 1990 census cohort (Panel C) are reasonably close to those estimated using the SRMP/CPS data.

The second item of note in Table 2.10 is the improvement in the relative wages of the 1980 cohort between 1980 and 1990. The difference between civilian and retiree weekly wages falls from 22 to 12 percent between 1980 and 1990. This convergence in retiree and civilian wages between 1980 and 1990 is at odds with the SRMP/CPS analysis presented earlier which shows little or no movement in relative wages between 1980 and 1995. The 1980 census figures, however, could be affected by the recession of the early 1980s. Retirees entering the civilian labor market at that time may have been particularly likely to take jobs with low wages. The fact that the relative weekly wages of the 1970 cohort falls to –0.17 in 1980 and then increases to –0.100 in 1990 also suggests that retirees (and perhaps other individuals with low job tenure) may have been particularly vulnerable to economic downturns.

To summarize, the data on retiree earnings available in the DRS, CPS, and U.S. Census seem to indicate that the oldest retirees in the SRMP overestimated their YOR earnings. SRMP earnings estimates made for more-recent years of retirement and in 1995, on the other hand, are generally consistent with those found in these other data sources. This implies that Table 2.4 may exaggerate the decline in relative retiree earnings over time. Based on the earnings reports of the SRMP retirees, one would conclude that relative retiree earnings in the year of retirement fell by 22 percentage points between the 1971 and 1974 and 1990 and 1994 cohorts. Based on the CPS-alone sample, however, one would conclude that relative retiree earnings fell by only 8 percentage points.

The recall bias evident in the SRMP also draws into question whether the SRMP data is underestimating the relative wage growth of retirees. Only the census permits a comparable analysis of relative wage growth, however, and the findings there also suggest retirees' wages gain little relative to civilian wages over time.

A NON-PARAMETRIC ANALYSIS OF RELATIVE WAGE GROWTH

So far, this analysis of relative retiree-civilian wages has proceeded by essentially comparing the mean wages of retirees and civilians conditional on various characteristics such as age and education. Focusing on a comparison of means can obscure the degree to which retirees move up or down the civilian wage distribution if the civilian wage distribution itself is changing at the same time. The 1970s and 1980s in fact witnessed a dramatic change in the civilian wage distribution as the difference between earnings at the top and those at the bottom of the distribution widened substantially. Many potential explanations exist for the sharp rise in civilian wage inequality over these decades, although increasing returns to skills, both measurable and immeasurable, are thought to be an important factor (Juhn, Murphy, and Pierce, 1993).

In an environment of rising civilian wage inequality, retirees entering the civilian labor market in relatively low-paying jobs could see their wages fall relative to the mean, even if their relative position within the distribution remains the same. Similarly, retirees entering the civilian labor market in relatively high-paying jobs could see their wages rise relative to the mean even in they did not advance at all within the distribution. This point has been made in the immigration literature by LaLonde and Topel (1990) and most recently by Lubotsky (1999).[20]

A comparison of mean wages over time is certainly instructive and provides one measure of how retirees fare relative to their civilian counterparts. But, the question posed in the literature to a large extent has been to what extent do retirees advance within the civilian

---

[20]Another way of stating this point is that the comparison of wage growth over time based on observable characteristics does not account for the possibility that the price of both observable and unobservable characteristics (or omitted variables) may be changing over time. To the extent that observable and unobservable characteristics differ between civilians and retirees, this misspecification can bias these estimates of wage convergence.

wage distribution over time. That is, if they first enter the civilian labor market at the 30th percentile of the wage distribution, do they tend to move upward toward the median (50th percentile) of the distribution as they gain civilian labor market experience?

It is conceivable that the pooled regression analysis earlier in this chapter understates this movement because it does not account for increasing civilian wage inequality. Take, for example, a retiree who enters the civilian labor market at the 30th percentile of the civilian wage distribution and ten years later has advanced to the 40th percentile. By this measure, I would argue that the retiree improved his relative position in the civilian labor market over those ten years. If the difference in wages between the mean of the civilian wage distribution and the 40th percentile increased markedly over that time, however, it could be the case that the retiree's position relative to mean wages did not change at all. In this case, the preceding analysis would indicate no movement in relative retiree wages over the ten-year period when in fact the retiree moved up in the distribution by ten percentile points. Relative to civilians with wages at the mean of the distribution, the retiree is no better off than he was ten years ago, but relative to civilians with wages below the 40th percentile of the distribution, he is better off.

An alternative way to examine the civilian wage growth of military retirees is to compare their position within the civilian wage distribution both in the year of retirement and in 1995. To do this, I pare down the pooled regression model presented earlier by conditioning wages only on year, age, and education. I divide age at retirement (37 to 50) into seven categories, age in 1995 into 14 categories, and education into three categories. Table 2.11 reports the proportion of retirees who fell (–), stayed in the same place (No change), or rose (+) within their respective civilian wage distributions between year of retirement and 1995 by cohort.[21]

Table 2.11 indicates a substantial amount of movement within the civilian wage distribution over time, movement that is masked in the

---

[21]Each retiree is assigned to a specific civilian wage distribution based on his year of retirement, education at retirement, age at retirement, and age in 1995. The civilian wage distribution is divided into five percentile increments.

Table 2.11

**Change in Retiree's Position Within the Civilian Wage Distribution
Between Year of Retirement and 1995**

| Retiree Cohort | Change in Percentile | | | All |
	(−)	No change	(+)	
A. Frequency				
1971–74	0.51	0.04	0.44	—
1975–79	0.48	0.08	0.44	—
1980–84	0.43	0.10	0.48	—
1985–89	0.40	0.15	0.46	—
1990–94	0.43	0.24	0.33	—
B. Magnitude of Change				
1971–74	−0.33	0	0.29	−0.04
1975–79	−0.32	0	0.29	−0.03
1980–84	−0.26	0	0.25	0.01
1985–89	−0.19	0	0.22	0.02
1990–94	−0.14	0	0.17	−0.003

NOTES: Civilian wages are distributed in five percentile increments. Civilian distribution is defined by year, age, and education.
SOURCES: 1996 SRMP and 1972 to 1996 March CPS.

regression analyses presented earlier in this chapter. The monthly wages of more than half of retirees separating between 1971 and 1974, for example, fell within the civilian wage distribution, while the monthly wages of 44 percent of these retirees rose within the civilian wage distribution (see Panel A in Table 2.11). The average decline within the distribution was 33 percentile points, while the average rise was 29 percentile points (see Panel B). Subsequent cohorts exhibit a similar pattern, although fewer retirees in these cohorts move up or down in the distribution and, for those that do, the magnitude of this movement is less pronounced. Consistent with earlier results, the overall average movement within the distribution is less than five percentile points for all cohorts.

In order to capture the effect of growing dispersion in the civilian wage distribution, I conducted the following thought experiment: What would retirees earn on average in 1995 if they maintained the same relative position within the civilian wage distribution that they had upon retirement?[22] In Table 2.12, I report the mean difference in retiree and civilian log wages by cohort calculated as follows: For all possible combinations of the set of characteristics defined by year of retirement, age, and education, I calculate

$$\Psi = \sum_k \left(f_k^r - f_k^c \right) \cdot y_k \tag{7}$$

where f_k^r is the density of retirees at the kth percentile of the civilian wage distribution, f_k^c is similarly defined for civilians, and y_k is the monthly log wage at the kth percentile of the civilian wage distribution. Thus, Ψ is the difference in the weighted average of retiree and civilian wages given a civilian wage distribution defined by year, age, and education. I then take a weighted average of Ψ where the weights represent the frequency of retirees with a given set of characteristics. I use a similar procedure in calculating Ψ using 1995 wages of retirees and civilians (see the column labeled Actual in Table 2.12).

Columns (1) and (2) of Table 2.12 reveal a pattern similar to that found in Table 2.4. Relative wages of recent retirees are far lower

Table 2.12

Mean Difference in Retiree-Civilian Log Wages, by Retiree Cohort: Accounting for the Effect of Wage Inequality

		1995		
Retiree Cohort	YOR (1)	Actual (2)	Counter-factual (3)	Rate of Relative Growth (2)–(3)
1971–74	−0.06	−0.05	−0.10	0.05
1975–79	−0.11	−0.07	−0.20	0.13
1980–84	−0.08	−0.10	−0.12	0.02
1985–89	−0.15	−0.15	−0.20	0.05
1990–94	−0.23	−0.24	−0.27	0.03

SOURCES: 1996 SRMP and 1972 to 1996 March CPS.

---

[22]This is the same thought experiment conducted by LaLonde and Topel (1990). Table 2.12 is organized in the same way as Table 7 in their study.

both in 1995 and in year of retirement than those of earlier retiree cohorts. Some differences exist in the results shown in Tables 2.4 and 2.12, which most likely reflect differences in controls (Table 2.4 controls for a wider range of covariates) and the fact that the results shown in Table 2.4 impose strong functional form assumptions on the relationship between retiree status and wages (that is, linearity). The results of Table 2.12 are derived non-parametrically and therefore are free of such assumptions.

Column (3) in Table 2.12 reports estimates of the difference between retiree and civilian wages assuming retirees remained at the same point of the civilian wage distribution in 1995 as when they first entered the civilian labor market. The results indicate that changes in the civilian wage distribution between YOR and 1995 affected the measure of relative wage growth between retirees and civilians. The 1971 to 1974 cohort, for example, entered the civilian labor market with wages 6 percent lower than civilian wages. By 1995, that difference was essentially unchanged at 5 percent. Column (3) shows, however, that had these retirees maintained their relative position within the civilian wage distribution between year of retirement and 1995, they would have earned wages 10 percent lower than mean civilian wages.

Thus, accounting for changes in the wage distribution, the wages of retirees actually grew relative to civilian wages by 5 percentage points. The same is true of later cohorts. Failing to account for changes in the civilian wage distribution causes an understatement of the wage growth of retirees of between four and ten percentage points. Taken together, these results imply greater movement in relative retiree wages than is suggested by the analysis of Table 2.4. This movement, though, is still much lower than that implied by earlier research on military retirees.

SUMMARY

Three principle observations emerge from the analyses presented in this chapter: (1) the civilian wages of military retirees generally lie below the wages of observationally similar civilians; (2) the civilian wages of military retirees grow relative to the wages of observationally similar civilians over the course of the retirees' second careers but not nearly as much as that implied by earlier research; and (3) civilian wages of military retirees upon separation have declined relative to civilian wages over time.

Recall bias in the SRMP probably exaggerates the extent to which relative retiree earnings have fallen across cohorts. It may also lead to underestimating the degree to which the wages of retirees grow relative to civilian wages with years in the civilian labor market. The analysis using census data, though, also points to low levels of retiree wage growth. Finally, the analysis in this chapter finds that rising civilian wage inequality partially masks the advances retirees make over the course of their second careers.

Chapter Three

ACCOUNTING FOR LOW RETIREE EARNINGS

How the data on relative retiree earnings presented in Chapter Two are interpreted depends critically on whether one believes the appropriate comparison is being made between civilians and retirees. For example, whether it is surprising that the wages of recent retirees lie 32 percent below mean civilian wages conditional on age, education, race, marital status, occupation, and geographic location depends upon whether this conditional mean of the civilian wage distribution is thought to be an appropriate reference point for retiree wages. It may be that, even conditional on these observed characteristics, differences in the abilities of military retirees and their civilian counterparts, and in the effort retirees and their counterparts expend in the civilian labor market, drive observed differences in civilian earnings.

This chapter explores a number of possible reasons why one might expect military retirees to earn relatively low earnings in their second careers. The discussion does not rely on formal tests, but rather presents an array of evidence using survey responses to a variety of subjective questions posed in the SRMP.

DO RETIREES THINK THEY EARN FAIR WAGES?

While formally controlling for unobserved differences in ability and effort is beyond the scope of this report, one can nevertheless make use of the answers to a number of subjective questions asked in the SRMP about the civilian labor market experiences of retirees to address this issue. One such question in the SRMP is as follows: "Overall, how much has being a military retiree helped or hindered your chances of getting a wage or salary comparable to civilian peers?" This question effectively asks retirees to compare themselves with a peer group of their own choosing rather than a peer group defined by the researcher.

The percentage of retirees who claim that being a military retiree hindered their chances of earning a wage comparable to their civilian peers ranges from a low of 17 percent in the 1971 to 1974 cohort to a high of 30 percent in the 1990 to 1994 cohort (see Table 3.1).[1] This strongly suggests that retirees do not view the mean of the civilian wage distribution as their reference point. For example, 70 percent of the 1990 to 1994 cohort earn wages below median civilian wages (conditional on age and education). The fact that only 30 percent of retirees think that their military career hindered their chance of earning a comparable wage suggests that their peers for the most part also earn wages below the median. Moreover, 91 percent of respondents report being satisfied with their civilian life and 90 percent report being satisfied with their military career. It is doubtful that these retirees would report such high levels of satisfaction if they thought their civilian wages were lagging far behind those of their peers.

CONTROLLING FOR VETERAN STATUS

It is of considerable interest that controlling for veteran status in the civilian population does not significantly alter the results of these analyses (see Table 3.2). That is, one observes the same pattern in relative retiree wages if the civilian comparison group is restricted to just veterans. In so doing, one presumably controls for factors that led both retirees and veterans with less than 20 years of service to enlist in the military in the first place (for example, both populations perceived the military to be a better opportunity than the civilian labor market when they first enlisted). Clearly, there remain important unobserved differences between retirees and other veterans, but controlling for veteran status perhaps reduces the scope for variation in ability to drive the differences observed in civilian wages.

---

[1]All statistics on subjective well-being, schooling, training, and transferability reported in this chapter are for the sample of retirees as presented in Table 2.4 in Chapter Two.

Table 3.1

Subjective Assessments of Well-Being Among Retirees (Percentage of Respondents)

Retiree Cohort	Military Career Hindered Chance of Earning Comparable Civilian Wages	Satisfied with Civilian Life	Satisfied with Military Career	Standard of Living Better Now than When in Military	Doing as Well as or Better than Civilian Peers	Proportion with 1995 Wages Below Median Civilian Wages[a]
1971–74	17	97	91	95	89	48
1975–79	22	95	90	92	83	49
1980–84	25	93	89	90	80	51
1985–89	25	91	91	85	76	58
1990–94	30	86	89	75	69	70

[a]Proportion conditional on age and education.

NOTE: Sample is as defined as in Table 2.4.

SOURCE: 1996 SRMP.

Table 3.2

Log Wage Gap in Year of Retirement and 1995, by Retiree Cohort: Veterans Only

Retiree Cohort	All Retirees	
	YOR	1995
1971–74	0.002	0.031
	(0.026)	(0.041)
1975–79	−0.084	−0.065
	(0.014)	(0.027)
1980–84	−0.059	−0.071
	(0.013)	(0.022)
1985–89	−0.145	−0.145
	(0.013)	(0.020)
1990–94	−0.255	−0.302
	(0.013)	(0.020)

NOTES: Civilian population restricted to veterans only. Log wage gap represents coefficient on retiree dummy in regression of log monthly wages on age, education, race, marital status, occupation, and private/public employment. Regressions are estimated separately by retiree cohort. Source: 1996 SRMP and 1972 to 1996 March CPS.

THE EFFECT OF RETIREE PENSION INCOME ON EFFORT EXPENDED IN THE CIVILIAN LABOR MARKET

Military retirees' access to pension income could affect their supply of effort in the labor market. In theory, this pension income would tend to cause retirees to consume more leisure, whether it be in the form of fewer work hours or less effort on the job, than their civilian peers. In the SRMP data, retirees report working about the same number of hours and weeks as civilians, but it is possible that retirees deliberately choose jobs that require less effort and responsibility than they are capable of and therefore earn lower wages by choice. More generally, retirees may choose jobs with a bundle of characteristics that emphasize non-pecuniary over pecuniary returns.[2]

Whereas on average the wages of retirees in their first civilian job fall below their military wages in their final year of service, the addition of pension income brings their total civilian compensation above

---

[2]More-detailed analysis of the occupational choice of military retirees would be a fruitful avenue for future research.

military compensation in most cases. As shown in Figure 3.1, civilian earnings plus pension is equal to or exceeds basic pay plus special pays in every case except for officers retiring between 1971 and 1979.[3] Only 20 percent of retirees claimed their standard of living in 1996 was worse than just before retiring from the military (see Table 3.1).

If we add pension income to retiree civilian wages, the 1995 wage gap as reported in Table 2.4 turns positive for all cohorts. Thus, even for the most recent retiree cohorts, total retiree earnings exceed average earnings of observationally comparable civilians. This may help explain why nearly 80 percent of retirees report that they are doing as well or better economically than their civilian peers despite the fact that nearly 60 percent earn wages substantially below median civilian wages.

Differences in effort could also help explain why one does not observe the wages of retirees catching up with civilian wages as they gain civilian labor market experience. The availability of pension income, for example, might influence not only the type of job retirees initially select but also their motivation to excel in their jobs and advance beyond their civilian peers. Hence, pension income could affect not only the initial level of retiree wages but the relative growth in retiree wages as well.

SKILL TRANSFERABILITY AND CIVILIAN WAGES

It may also be the case that the assumptions underlying the theory of why retiree wages might be expected to converge with civilian wages over time do not hold. The principal hypothesis of wage convergence assumes first that the reason retirees enter the civilian labor market with relatively low wages is because their military skills do not transfer completely to the civilian sector. The hypothesis then assumes that retirees respond to this skill deficit by acquiring civilian labor market skills at a faster rate than civilians so that their wages gradually catch up with the wages of their peers. In regard to the second

---

[3]Total military compensation could be higher than what is estimated here because the value of on-base housing and federal and state tax advantages are not included in these estimates.

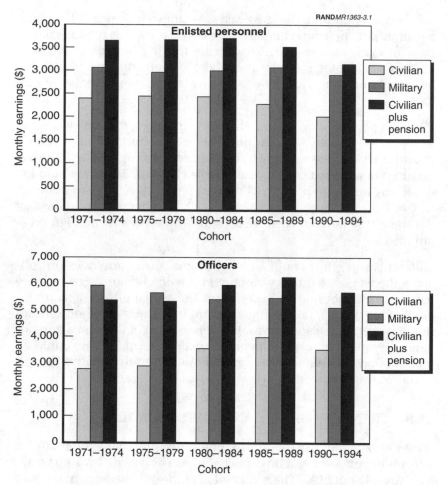

NOTES: Military pay includes basic pay plus special pay plus allowances.
Between 1983 and 1994, special pay and allowances are calculated within rank and
year of service cells. Between 1971 and 1982, special pay and allowances are
approximated using the average ratio of special pay plus allowances to basic pay for
the period 1983 to 1987. Military pay does not include the value of on-base housing
and federal and state tax advantages.

SOURCES: 1996 SRMP, Department of Defense (1996), and 1983 to 1996
JMPS data.

**Figure 3.1—Military and Civilian Earnings upon Separation, by Retiree
Cohort (1995 Dollars)**

point, some evidence exists in the SRMP that retirees enter a period of relatively intense skill acquisition when they first separate from the military.

In terms of formal schooling, 14 percent of SRMP respondents report attending school full time or part time as their main activity immediately following separation. According to self-reports, 52 percent of retirees with a high-school-level education upon separation attended some college in the subsequent years, and 8 percent completed a four-year degree or more. Among those with some college upon separation, 20 percent went on to complete a four-year degree, and among college graduates, 20 percent completed a higher degree. There is some evidence on training as well; 20 percent of SRMP respondents reported that they pursued training of some variety in order to qualify themselves for their first civilian job and another 20 percent received training while employed in their first job. This schooling and training apparently did not result in substantially higher wage growth for retirees, however.

The idea that military skills do not necessarily translate well to the civilian sector has been emphasized in much of the empirical work addressing the civilian wages of veterans (Warner and Asch, 1995). Goldberg and Warner (1987), for example, find that veterans who trained in military occupations that *a priori* appear to offer transferable skills (electronics or medical training versus combat arms) earn wages more comparable to those of civilians. The SRMP, though, does not offer much evidence of a large skill mismatch between military and civilian occupations.

More than three-quarters of SRMP respondents (77 percent) stated that their military experience was valuable or very valuable to their civilian careers and only 25 percent of SRMP respondents felt that their military career had hampered their civilian career (see Table 3.1). The SRMP also asked what percentage of military skills were useful in the retirees' first job; 55 percent of respondents reported percentages higher than 50 in the first job, although it is notable that enlistees report lower levels of transferability than retirees (see Table 3.3). The relatively short job search of most retirees (57 percent had full-time jobs lined up before they actually separated and over half of those who did not have jobs lined up found full-time work within the

Table 3.3

Transferability of Skills by Rank and Year of Retirement (Percentage of Respondents)

Retiree Cohort	Less than 25% of Military Skills Relevant to First Civilian Job		Less than 50% of Military Skills Relevant to First Civilian Job		Military Experience Not Valuable to Civilian Career		Military Career Hindered Chance of Finding Full-Time Employment	
	Enlistees	Officers	Enlistees	Officers	Enlistees	Officers	Enlistees	Officers
1971–74	38	37	50	49	26	27	6	11
1975–79	39	32	54	49	25	22	9	11
1980–84	34	22	48	38	25	17	9	10
1985–89	38	21	51	37	29	17	12	15
1990–94	43	23	59	38	39	19	16	19

NOTE: Sample defined as in Table 2.4.
SOURCE: 1996 SRMP.

first six months of separation) is also inconsistent with the notion of a civilian labor market that does not value military skills.

Lastly, fewer than 15 percent of the SRMP sample indicated that military service hindered their ability to find full-time civilian employment (see Table 3.3). So, although it is certainly plausible that many retirees develop specific skills while in the military, it does not appear that this particular kind of skill development is a major limitation in finding gainful employment in the civilian sector.

Wage convergence is most frequently studied in the literature on immigration and job displacement. The parallels between the experience of immigrants and military retirees in the civilian labor market are dubious at best, primarily because whereas retirees may lack certain skills that are beneficial in the civilian labor market, this skill deficiency cannot be as significant as the challenge most immigrants face of acquiring a new language. The parallel with displaced workers, though, is more plausible. The literature on job displacement generally concludes that displaced workers experience wage losses on the order of 15 to 20 percent, even three to five years after displacement.

Jacobson, LaLonde, and Sullivan (1993) list a variety of reasons why the wages of displaced workers might fall permanently following displacement. In addition to the possibility that displaced workers lose firm-specific capital in the transition, the influence of union rules, efficiency wages, and deferred compensation could all act to depress the wages of middle-age individuals with low tenure. For example, it is commonly argued that firms pay older workers wages above their marginal product in an effort to retain workers in which the firm invested in earlier years. With no prior investment to protect, firms would be unwilling to pay comparable wages to retirees. Firms may also be unwilling to invest significant training resources in these individuals because the period over which such an investment could be recouped is relatively short.

DECLINING WAGES ACROSS SUCCESSIVE RETIREE COHORTS

There are a number of reasons, then, why retiree wages might not converge with civilian wages as a simple human capital model might predict. Perhaps a bigger puzzle is why the relative wages of retirees have fallen across successive cohorts. The SRMP analysis probably overstates this decline due to overreporting of initial earnings by older retirees, but the CPS and U.S. Census data on retirees also show a decline. Answers to two subjective questions in the SRMP are also suggestive of a potential decline in the relative position of retirees. The proportion of retirees who feel they are doing as well or better than their civilian peers fell from 0.89 to 0.69 between the 1971 to 1974 and 1990 to 1994 cohorts, and the proportion who feel their standard of living is better now than while in the military has fallen from 0.95 to 0.75 (see Table 3.1).

Two potential explanations for the decline in relative retiree wages immediately come to mind: (1) the overall quality of retirees has declined over time and (2) wages earned in the types of jobs available to retirees have declined over time. Upon closer examination, though, neither explanation is particularly satisfying. Scores on the Armed Forces Qualifying Test (AFQT) may be the best measure of quality. If nothing else, they are highly correlated with civilian earnings (see, for example, Neal and Johnson [1996]). But, by this measure, there was little change in the distribution of quality among enlistees in the SRMP. The proportion of enlistees scoring in AFQT categories I, II, and III ranged between 78 and 85 percent across cohorts.[4] To my knowledge, there is no other evidence that the quality of military personnel declined over this period.[5]

Even with constant quality, it could be that the decline in real wages in the lower half of the civilian wage distribution over the 1970s and 1980s depressed relative to retiree wages. If it is assumed that retirees entered the same types of civilian jobs in the early 1970s as in the early 1990s, but the wages paid for those jobs declined relative to

---

[4]A substantial amount of AFQT data is missing in the SRMP, although this is not correlated with year of retirement. Historical data on the AFQT scores of male accessions between 1958 and 1972, which roughly corresponds to the accession period of retirees in the SRMP, shows a small increase in the percentage of accessions with AFQT scores in categories I through III (59 percent in 1958 to 1963 to 73 percent in 1971 to 1972) (Karpinos, 1975).

[5]The most well-known decline in the quality of military recruits occurred between FY 1976 and 1980, when the DoD badly misnormed the AFQT and therefore mistakenly admitted large numbers of category IV enlistees (Angrist, 1998). This error, of course, occurred well after the SRMP population would have joined the military.

mean civilian wages, then one would observe declining relative re-tiree wages over that period. This is essentially the point made in Table 2.12 in Chapter Two, but in terms of levels not growth rates. This is a plausible explanation for the magnitude of the decline in relative retiree wages observed in the U.S. Census (about 10 percentage points). It is not a satisfactory explanation, however, if the SRMP/CPS analysis is taken as the baseline. There, the magnitude of the decline is nearly 25 percentage points.

Other potential explanations for the decline in relative retiree earn-ings include increasing returns to civilian experience and the rising importance of spousal income. It could be that the relative return to civilian experience vis-à-vis military experience increased between 1970 and 1994. Retirees separating in the early 1970s could secure jobs with wages comparable to those of civilians because their military experience earned the same return as civilian experience. By the early 1990s, the same level of military experience earned a lower relative return, so retirees are observed separating at that time earning wages well below mean civilian wages.

Another possibility for the decline in relative retiree earnings is that more-recent retirees are more likely to make civilian labor market decisions in concert with the labor market choices of their spouse. The rate of female labor force participation rose sharply over this pe-riod and therefore the likelihood that a given retiree's labor market choices would be constrained by a spouse's career has no doubt risen. If the retiree is no longer viewed as the household's primary earner, he may be more likely to settle for a relatively low-paying job and contribute more time to household production. Spousal income might also generate a wealth effect that causes more-recent retirees to consume more leisure, if not in fewer work hours then in less re-sponsibility or stress on the job.

Chapter Four

CONCLUSIONS

This report highlights several important features of the civilian labor market experience of military retirees. Contrary to a simple model of human capital accumulation and recent empirical research, the wages of military retirees do not grow appreciably faster than the wages of observationally similar civilians over the course of their civilian careers.

The research for this study, like the recent research on the earnings of immigrants, has emphasized the importance of controlling for cohort effects when making inferences about relative wage growth. The analysis in this report shows that, in fact, cohort effects are quite strong in the retiree population; more-recent retirees earn civilian wages that are considerably lower than those of retirees who separated from the military in the 1970s. Despite earning comparatively low wages, however, retirees seem to find the transition to civilian life to be fairly painless; they find full-time work quickly and report a high level of satisfaction with their civilian lives. Among the findings in this report, the apparent decline in relative retiree wages over the 1970s and 1980s is perhaps the most puzzling and deserving of future research.

Although this report offers a more-accurate depiction of the post-service earnings experience of military retirees than was previously available, it does not answer the important question of whether the military's current pension system is an efficient component of overall compensation in the sense that it accomplishes desired retention objectives at least cost. On observable grounds, it appears that military personnel suffer a considerable decline in wages upon separation, although they are more than compensated for that decline by their military pension. Borjas and Welch seem to think that this finding alone justifies a pension system with high payouts: "If retirees do not do very well during their second career, as the findings in this paper suggest, high-quality potential recruits will find a full-time civilian career more beneficial unless either the pension payment or earnings while in the service are adjusted upward to compensate for the relatively low postservice earnings" (Borjas and Welch, 1986, p. 312).

This conclusion is premature, I believe, without a deeper understanding of the true civilian labor market opportunities of military personnel. It is simply not known whether military service per se harms post-service earnings. Researchers have yet to credibly model the unobservable determinants of accession and reenlistment decisions in this population and therefore one cannot be certain what the civilian wages of retirees would have been had they separated at an earlier age or never joined the military at all. Moreover, one does not know the degree to which retirees curtail labor supply or personal effort as a result of their pension income. These are important questions that deserve further attention.

Of course, the design of an efficient pension system requires more than just an understanding of these two unknowns. Even if it turns out that most military personnel would have earned relatively low wages in the civilian labor market regardless of service, and that pension income has strong negative effects on post-service labor supply or effort, current pension expenditures can be justified on other grounds. Deferred compensation motivates work effort and creates appropriate incentives for high-quality personnel to reenlist and low-quality personnel to separate. Additionally, the pension system may reduce costs associated with involuntary and uncompensated separations that harm morale.

DERIVATION OF RETIREE STATUS FROM CENSUS DATA

The 1970, 1980, and 1990 U.S. Census includes questions on military service. Unfortunately, only the 1990 census specifically asked respondents to report years of service. Consequently, the analysis in Table 2.10 in Chapter Two uses information on periods of service, in combination with current military status and age, to code individuals as either a retiree or civilian.

Beginning with the 1970 census, I code all individuals between the ages of 40 and 44 not currently on active duty service but who reported serving during the Korean conflict (1950 to 1955) and the Vietnam era (1964 to 1975) as retirees.[1] It is unlikely that many of these individuals separated with less than 20 years of service because, by serving in both of these periods, they would have served a minimum of nine years and would have forgone a substantial amount of delayed compensation (pension income) by separating early.

I start with a group age 40 to 44 in 1970 because I want individuals who are likely to be recent entrants into the civilian labor market. I then code individuals between the ages of 50 and 54 in the 1980 census as retirees if they served between 1950 and 1955 and 1964 and 1975, did not serve between 1975 and 1980, and were not currently on active duty service. Finally, I code individuals age 60 to 64 in the 1990 census as retirees if they served between 1950 and 1955 and

---

[1] There is no indicator variable for service between 1955 and 1964 in the 1970 U.S. Census.

1964 and 1975, did not serve between 1975 and 1990, and were not currently on active duty service.

The aim with these sample restrictions is to create a synthetic cohort of retirees age 40 to 44 in 1970, age 50 to 54 in 1980, and age 60 to 64 in 1990. In addition to the problem that some of these individuals may have separated with fewer than 20 years of service, some of the age 50 to 54 and age 60 to 64 cohorts will have served between 1970 and 1975 whereas none of the age 40 to 44 cohort will have served in that period.[2] Thus, I cannot be certain that the 1980 and 1990 group is composed of the same individuals as the 1970 group. In fact, it is likely that average years of service are higher among individuals in the 1980 and 1990 groups because they could have served as many as five years after 1970.

These definitions yield retiree populations totaling 3.0, 4.9, and 5.2 percent of the male veteran population in 1970, 1980, and 1990, respectively. These percentages are comparable to the proportion of the veteran population receiving military pension income in the CPS.

I also examine a cohort of retirees age 40 to 44 in 1980. These individuals are coded as retirees if they served between 1955 and 1964, 1964 and 1975, and 1975 and 1980, but were not currently on active duty service. Individuals age 50 to 54 in 1990 who did not serve between 1980 and 1990 were then coded as retirees using the same criteria. This analysis is less likely to suffer from the problems noted in using the 1970 data, as mentioned earlier, because by serving in all three of these periods, the individuals' minimum years of service are somewhat higher (11 years versus 9 years) and there is no ambiguity about post-1980 service.

Finally, I examine a cohort of veterans age 40 to 44 in 1990 who are coded as retirees if they served between 1964 and 1975, 1975 and 1980, and 1980 and 1990, but were not currently on active duty service.

---

[2] The 1990 U.S. Census reports years of service and therefore it is possible to check whether retirees as defined in this appendix have 20 or more years of service. I find that 10 and 12 percent of the 1970 and 1980 retiree cohorts report having fewer than 20 years of service.

BIBLIOGRAPHY

Angrist, J., "Estimating the Labor Market Impact of Voluntary Military Service Using Social Security Data on Military Applicants," *Econometrica*, Vol. 66, No. 2, 1998, pp. 249–288.

_____, "Lifetime Earnings and the Vietnam Era Draft Lottery: Evidence from Social Security Records," *American Economic Review*, Vol. 80, No. 2, 1990, pp. 313–336.

_____, "Using the Draft Lottery to Measure the Effects of Military Service on Civilian Labor Market Outcomes," in R. Ehrenberg, ed., *Research in Labor Economics*, Greenwich, Conn.: JAI Press, 1989.

Angrist, J., and A. Krueger, "Why Do World War II Veterans Earn More Than Nonveterans?" *Journal of Labor Economics*, Vol. 12, No. 1, 1994, pp. 74–97.

Asch, B., and J. Warner, *A Policy Analysis of Alternative Military Retirement Systems*, Santa Monica, Calif.: RAND, MR-465-OSD, 1994.

Bollinger, C., "Measurement Error in the Current Population Survey: A Nonparametric Look," *Journal of Labor Economics*, Vol. 16, No. 3, 1998, pp. 576–594.

Borjas, G., "The Economics of Immigration," *Journal of Economic Literature*, Vol. 32, No. 4, 1994, pp. 1667–1717.

_____, "Assimilation, Changes in Cohort Quality, and the Earnings of Immigrants," *Journal of Labor Economics*, Vol. 3, No. 4, 1985, pp. 463–489.

Borjas, G., and F. Welch, "The Post-Service Earnings of Military Retirees." in C. Gilroy, ed., *Army Manpower Economics*, Boulder, Colo.: Westview Press, 1986.

_____, *A Review of Richard Cooper's "Military Retirees' Postservice Earnings and Employment,"* Santa Monica, Calif.: Unicon Research Corporation, 1983.

Boskin, M., E. Dulberger, R. Gordon, Z. Griliches, and D. Jorgenson, "Consumer Prices, the Consumer Price Index, and the Cost of Living," *Journal of Economic Perspectives*, Vol. 12, No. 1, 1998, pp. 3–26.

Bound, J., C. Brown, G. Duncan, and W. Rodgers, "Measurement Error in Cross-Sectional Longitudinal Labor Market Surveys: Results from Two Validation Studies," NBER Working Paper No. 2884, Cambridge, Mass: National Bureau of Economic Research, 1989.

Bound, J., and A. Krueger, "The Extent of Measurement Error in Longitudinal Earnings Data: Do Two Wrongs Make a Right?" *Journal of Labor Economics*, Vol. 9, No. 1, 1991, pp. 1–24.

Bryant, R., V. Samaranayake, and A. Wilhite, "The Effect of Military Service on the Subsequent Civilian Wage of the Post-Vietnam Veteran," *Quarterly Review of Economics and Finance*, Vol. 33, No. 1, 1993, pp. 15–31.

Cardell, S., D. Lamoreaux, E. Stromsdorfer, B. Wang, and G. Weeks, "The Post-Service Earnings of Military Retirees: A Comparison of the 1996 Retired Military Personnel Sample with a Statistically Comparable Sample from the March 1994 Current Population Survey," unpublished manuscript, Washington State University, 1997.

Chiswick, B., "The Effect of Americanization on the Earnings of Foreign-Born Men," *Journal of Political Economy*, Vol. 86, No. 5, 1978, pp. 81–87.

Cooper, R., *Military Retirees' Post-Service Earnings and Employment*, Santa Monica, Calif.: RAND, R-2493-MRAL, 1981.

Department of Defense, *Military Compensation Background Papers*, 5th ed., Washington, D.C.: U.S. Government Printing Office, 1996.

Gilroy, C., T. Daymont, P. Andrisani, and R. Phillips, "The Economic Returns to Military Service: Race-Ethnic Differences," *Social Science Quarterly*, Vol. 73, No. 2, 1992, pp. 340–359.

Goldberg, M., and J. Warner, "Military Experience, Civilian Experience, and the Earnings of Veterans," *Journal of Human Resources*, Vol. 22, No. 1, 1987, pp. 62–81.

Henry, R., and R. Reimer, "The 1996 Retired Military Personnel Survey," unpublished manuscript, Arlington, Va.: Defense Manpower Data Center, 1997.

Jacobson, L., R. LaLonde, and D. Sullivan, "Earnings Losses of Displaced Workers," *American Economic Review*, Vol. 83, No. 4, 1993, pp. 685–709.

Juhn, C., K. Murphy, and B. Pierce, "Wage Inequality and the Rise in Returns to Skill," *Journal of Political Economy*, Vol. 101, No. 3, 1993, pp. 410–442.

Karpinos, B., *AFQT: Historical Data (1958–72)*, Alexandria, Va.: Human Resources Research Organization, MR-76-1, 1975.

LaLonde, R., and R. Topel, "The Assimilation of Immigrants in the U.S. Labor Market," NBER Working Paper No. 3573, Cambridge, Mass.: National Bureau of Economic Research, 1990.

Lubotsky, D., "How Well Do Immigrants Assimilate into the U.S. Labor Market? A Longitudinal Analysis of Earnings, Self-Selection, and the Return to Skills," unpublished manuscript, Department of Economics, University of California, Berkeley, 1999.

Milgrom, P., "Employment Contracts, Influence Activities, and Efficient Organization Design," *Journal of Political Economy*, Vol. 96, No. 1, pp. 42–60, 1988.

Neal, D., and W. Johnson, "The Role of Premarket Factors in Black-White Wage Differences," *Journal of Political Economy*, Vol. 104, No. 5, 1996, pp. 869–895.

Pischke, J., "Measurement Error and Earnings Dynamics: Some Estimates from the PSID Validation Study," *Journal of Business and Economic Statistics*, Vol. 13, No. 3, 1995, pp. 305–314.

Pleeter, S., "Post-Retirement Military Income," unpublished manuscript, Office of the Assistant Secretary of Defense, Force Management Policy, Arlington, Va.: Department of Defense, 1995.

Riemer, R., and D. Lamoreaux, "The 1996 Survey of Retired Military Personnel: Statistical Methodology Report," unpublished manuscript, Arlington, Va.: Defense Manpower Data Center, 1997.

U.S. Government Printing Office, *Career Compensation for the Uniformed Services*, Washington, D.C., 1948.

Warner, J., and B. Asch, "The Economics of Military Manpower," in K. Hartley and T. Sandler, eds., *Handbook of Defense Economics*, Amsterdam: Elsevier Science, 1995.

Warner, J., and C. Simon, "Matchmaker, Matchmaker: The Effect of Old Boy Networks on Job Match Quality, Earnings, and Tenure," *Journal of Labor Economics*, Vol. 10, No. 3, 1992, pp. 306–330.